The Dynamics of Balsa

Edited by

Liz Niven

and

Brian Whittingham

with Michel Byrne (Gaelic Adviser)

Association for Scottish Literary Studies

Association for Scottish Literary Studies
Department of Scottish Literature, 7 University Gardens
University of Glasgow, Glasgow G12 8QH
www.asls.org.uk

First published 2007

© Association for Scottish Literary Studies
and the individual contributors

British Library Cataloguing in Publication Data

A CIP record for this book is available
from the British Library

ISBN: 978-0-948877-77-3

The Association for Scottish Literary Studies
acknowledges the support of the Scottish Arts Council
towards the publication of this book

Typeset by AFS Image Setters Ltd, Glasgow

Printed by Bell & Bain Ltd, Glasgow

CONTENTS

INTRODUCTION

Welcome to this year's *New Writing Scotland*, which has now reached its quarter-century milestone. The intriguing title was conjured up from that unexpected dynamic discovered as we pored through one thousand manuscripts. In this case, one thousand from 440 authors. A bumper crop. Those large brown cardboard boxes lived with us for quite some time as we dipped and read, dipped and read until it was time to swap boxes and repeat the procedure.

Poems, prose pieces, extracts from plays and novels, a juxtaposition emerged and with it that deceptive quality with the properties of balsa wood, a wonderful balance of apparent lightness with an inherent strength.

There are striking and original voices, the central criteria for selection. As expected with an anthology of new writing, there's sometimes further drafting possible. 'When is a poem or story finished?' is a question that will always be asked as long as writers are writing. Again, if the turn of phrase was original, the observation unique and the personal expressed, it was selected.

Judging anonymously, we had no idea if we were selecting weel-kent names or first-time writers. So even after reading hundreds of scripts, the final published book was as much a surprise to the editors as to the readers, which is just as it should be. It means there's no bias, no nepotism, just the writing which appealed most to the editorial eye and ear of two individuals.

Amongst the resulting 44 manuscripts – 16 prose pieces and 28 poems – there's comedy: check out 'The American Hit Man'; there's tragedy, in poems such as 'The Doctor Smoked a Pipe'; and there's the whole gamut of emotions represented in between.

This year, we have remained in Scotland for most of the time, with an occasional venture out to China, Eastern Europe, the world of the future, or, more often, to the geography of the heart and the head.

We've fair enjoyed reading, debating and ultimately selecting this year's crop of new writing from Scotland. We hope you will find stories and poems which appeal to you whether urban, rural or in the landscape of the mind.

Dynamics can happen anywhere, any way and in a variety of voices in contemporary Scotland. Enjoy!

Liz Niven
Brian Whittingham

NEW WRITING SCOTLAND 26

The twenty-sixth volume of *New Writing Scotland* will be published in summer 2008. Submissions are invited from writers resident in Scotland or Scots by birth or upbringing. All forms of writing are invited: autobiography and memoirs; creative responses to events and experiences; drama; graphic artwork (monochrome only); poetry; political and cultural commentary and satire; short fiction; travel writing; or any other creative prose may be submitted, but not full-length plays or novels, though self-contained extracts are acceptable. The work must be neither previously published nor accepted for publication and may be in any of the languages of Scotland.

Submissions should be typed, double-spaced, on one side of the paper only and the sheets secured at the top-left corner. Prose pieces should carry an approximate word-count. **You should provide a covering letter, clearly marked with your name and address. Please do not put your name or other details on the individual works.** If you would like to receive an acknowledgement of receipt of your manuscript, please enclose a stamped addressed postcard. If you would like to be informed if your submission is unsuccessful, or if you would like your submissions returned, you should enclose a stamped addressed envelope with sufficient postage. Submissions should be sent by **30 September 2007**, in an A4 envelope, to the address below. We are sorry but we cannot accept submissions by fax or e-mail.

Please be aware that we have limited space in each edition, and therefore shorter pieces are more suitable – although longer items of exceptional quality may still be included. A maximum length of 3,500 words is suggested. Please send no more than a single prose work and no more than four poems.

ASLS
Department of Scottish Literature
7 University Gardens
University of Glasgow
Glasgow G12 8QH, Scotland

Tel +44 (0)141 330 5309
www.asls.org.uk

Keith Aitchison

A CLOSE SHAVE

It was a cheap hotel at the working end of town, one of those recommended by other travellers on the long haul across the Middle East. No air-conditioning, certainly no en-suite, but a good bit of English spoken, clean sheets, a decent working shower on each floor, the minimum number of bedbugs and no attempts to rip you off.

I climbed a flight of steps from the hot street bustle of people and noisy vehicles and burdened donkeys, a smell of diesel fumes and drains tainting the air, seeking a room on the morning shadow side where dawn would not rouse me to admire it painting white walls a fleeting rose and pink.

I had been in the hills, needed a rest. Three days on the road, or rather two days on sand and another on gravel before the final twenty kilometres rolling luxuriously along the concrete highway stitching together mountains and deserts with the river valleys and hard-worked stony fields of this country.

The hotel clerk didn't have as much English as I'd heard, but tried attentively to follow my blend of English and German laced with those few words of his own tongue I had picked up in the mountains, his patient courtesy concealing behind horn-rimmed spectacles any thoughts that what I really needed was not difficult conversation concerning morning shadow but a good wash: my face grey with a fine patina of dust, hair grimy and knotted, clothes sweat-stained and crumpled, four days' growth of beard on my face.

He had no single room available at my price, but if I was prepared to share, there was a bed in a twin, the other taken by an American, although he wasn't there at the moment. And it wasn't clear where he was or what had happened or might happen: something which failed the language barrier and in the end could only be expressed as a resigned shrug – he might return soon; he might not be back at all.

Wherever he'd gone, his gear had been left scrambled across a disordered bed, clothes mainly, but also an empty water-bottle, towel and shaving brush and a tattered paperback copy of *Nostromo*. Curious, but I put my rucksack

down and went for a shower, its tepid water peeling away
the dust to swirl muddily around my feet.

I rinsed my clothes, working the worst stains with a
thinning cake of soap which alone delayed permanent
grubbiness, shaved and then went back to the room and a
tray of black tea and flat bread the clerk had sent up to me.
A lump of sugar chewed with bread brought back the taste
of breakfast cereal, and so memories of home, Glasgow's
cool rain rather than the burning bare sky outside, and I
relaxed, dozed.

An annoyed donkey brayed from the street and I opened
my eyes to the whitewashed wall and a minute splash of
red marking where an unwise mosquito had lingered after
feeding. Evening had come, the last sunlight spilling drowsy
heat into the room and sparkling on motes of dust. My eyes
closed once more.

When the sun's brilliance had gone and a brief dusk
was sinking to darkness, the creak of an opening door woke
me again.

He turned on the weak electric light, casting a pool of
yellow illumination. Younger than me, shortish fair hair
and a creased bush shirt which might once have been
expensive.

I raised myself on my elbow and he looked at me out
of an exhausted face.

'You're the Englishman,' he said. 'I'm Allan.'

'Iain,' I introduced myself. 'And Scots. You'll be
American.'

'Canadian,' he corrected in his turn and smiled wearily,
'I guess we both get used to being taken for something
else.'

'What's the town like?'

'Couple of old mosques, if you like mosques,' his voice
held no enthusiasm. 'Some good stuff in the bazaar – leather
jackets, brasswork and so on. You can eat in the hotel
restaurant without it necessarily giving you the shits, but no
beer, of course. Best thing, the airport's open again, thank
Jesus.'

'You leaving?'

'Twelve hours. All the way home, if I make the
connections. Maybe that's why they let me go at last.'

'Let you go?' I sat up.

'I've been in the slammer for two days.' Allan put his hands through his hair, his face streaked with remembered bewilderment.

'What happened?'

'Nothing! Well, nothing to do with me,' he nodded to where I sat. 'The last guy in that bed, it's all down to him, the bastard. Poor bastard.'

I waited, but he said nothing more for a space, looking through the window at the dimly-lit street, giving one long sigh.

Tinny music sounded from a radio outside, high notes and cadences swooping against the background murmur of voices as men gathered at their doors to enjoy the evening cool. The smell of mutton roasting over glowing charcoal wafted distractingly into our room.

'His name's Joe,' Allan finally continued. 'American, from Arkansas. Big black beard, seemed a nice guy, friendly, the sort you take to straight off, you know? We ate together a few times. He was waiting for the airport to open so he could fly out home. Just like me.

'He'd been out here some months – so he said, anyway – and gave up shaving early. Now he looked a bit like one of those American patriarchs you see in old photographs of the West. Of course, they're not the ones with beards now; it's what's left of the counter-culture, isn't it.'

'Not here, though,' I remarked. 'A beard's almost compulsory.'

'Yes, but Joe was heading back to the States, and the beard worried him. He thought – he *said* he thought – it would earn him a hard time at US Customs, especially as his passport photo dated from Eleventh Grade, and he hardly looked much like that anymore.

'His flight was booked for the next day, and he was sitting where you are now, pulling nervously at his beard.

' "You won't know what our Customs and Immigration are like," he told me. "Blue collar and most of them right-wing enough to frighten the Ku Klux Klan. If they don't take to how you look, they shake you down and trash your stuff. It's only the Land of the Free if you've got a suit and a tie and a good shave. Anything else, you're fair game, a hippy, maybe a subversive."

'Joe inspected his beard in the mirror, edgily combing

his fingers through the strands to see how it looked when a bit neater.

' "I might as well have a target on my chest," he complained finally. "They'll pick me out the moment I get off the plane."

' "Get rid of it," I suggested the obvious solution. "Sure, you'll look paler underneath, but that's got to be easier."

' "I guess that might be best." Joe looked enquiringly at me. "I've left the razor someplace. Can I borrow yours?"

'I didn't think anything of it.' Allan shrugged. 'He trimmed his hair, shaved the beard away, even brought out a tie, so he seemed really different, more like a young Republican intern working in Congress, packed and left for the airport. I didn't think anything of it, not until the cops came for me.'

'Why?' I still couldn't see it.

'They thought I might be involved!' Allan exclaimed bitterly. 'Though they didn't say why till much later. At least they treated me well, by their standards, anyway. Nobody beat me up or anything. They kept me fed and gave me a cell to myself.'

Then he shuddered as if an icy wind had closed on him.

'Wasn't a picnic, though. Just a couple of old blankets and two rusty tins, one to piss in, the other with water and you can bet they get mixed up. And mosquitoes. Lots of mosquitoes. Close the window and suffocate in the heat. Open it and the bugs get in to eat you. Some choice, huh? They questioned me over and over again. And they had a smart guy on it, the second day. Must have brought him in from the capital. He spoke good English as you or me, wore a suit, very neat, looked like a Toronto businessman.

'Questions, questions: where did I meet Joe; was I sure; where did we eat together; where did I meet him; remind me – what time was that; where did you meet; had I met him before; didn't you say something different last time you answered? Was I certain; did I realise how important it was I got this right; didn't I know this was about me as much as Joe?

'I guess I finally convinced him when he showed me Joe's holdall with ten kilos of hash sewed into the lining, and I flipped out. Anyway, he told me why they'd brought me in, and let me go.'

Allan sank back on his bed and stared at the ceiling.

'Ten kilos,' I whistled. 'What do they hand out for that?'

'I'm told it's a year for each kilo,' he shuddered again. 'My God, ten years in one of those cells. Or maybe worse. My God.'

'Well,' I said comfortingly, 'you're not in the frame. And you're flying home in a few hours. Forget it.'

'Right,' he allowed himself a smile. 'And I've only got to collect a couple of things – a leather jacket, and a piece of blue lapis in silver, for my girl. Pair of leather slippers. All I've lost is my razor – that's evidence, apparently.'

Allan's face darkened, took on a frown.

'It's what got me the two days in jail,' he grimaced. 'They'd been watching Joe for some time, ever since he got his stash, and they knew he'd be flying out when the airport opened again. He nearly got past them because they were watching for his great black beard, but he turned up clean-shaven, which almost threw them, but not enough. It was plain that he hadn't been to a barber – a few nicks and uneven sideburns told them that, but there wasn't a razor in his gear, so that was another question and, as having a shave is no crime, he told them. Which is when they decided to pull me in to see whether I should join Joe in whatever hell-hole he's bound for now.'

After he'd washed, Allan joined me for a meal downstairs in the hotel restaurant, kebabs in buttery rice with sugared lemon to drink. Then we went out into the busy streets where men in turbans or skullcaps and women in the drab concealment of chadors were enjoying these few, relatively comfortable, hours, every shop open, noise and music everywhere, each merchant at his door and vigilant for custom, chaikhanas and restaurants doing good business into the deep of the night.

Allan's purchases were waiting at a small shop down a bazaar alleyway, the owner an Uzbek, I thought, round, cheerful face with a fringe of white hair, quick eyes slanting with memories of Central Asia.

We brought the packages back to the hotel and Allan unwrapped them to check more closely if they were okay. His brown leather jacket lined in silk, black buttons and broad, flapped pockets. Beads of polished blue lapis in the grasp of a silver pendant.

Slippers thick-soled and bright with wax.

He lifted them and sniffed at the stitches joining soles to uppers, glanced at me, shyly. And I knew.

'That's *your* stash in there, isn't it? In the soles.'

'About a half-kilo. They'll never find it, quite safe.'

'That's not a new trick. You're taking a chance, both ends of the flight.'

'But isn't that a reason we come out here? The sort of risk we can't get at home?'

'There's something in that,' I acknowledged.

Allan glanced at his watch and rubbed his bristled jaw.

'Think I'll have a last shower. You know, my girl's meeting me at Lester Pearson tomorrow. I don't want to look like a tramp.'

He turned to me hopefully, innocently. Or maybe not innocently.

'Could you help me out? Could I borrow your razor?'

Kirsten Anderson

THE PIGEON

Do you want to know the best bit? I hated pigeons back then. I hated everything if truth be told but I'd reserved a little pocket of ill-will in my gut just for the pigeons living under that bridge. I'd walked under it Friday after Friday for 20 years and every single time, I'd look up to the rafters and spit out a bit of venom at the congealed green and white shit they'd splattered all over the concrete. Fucking wee bastards, I'd mutter. And now I'm sitting here saying one of those fucking wee bastards changed my life. Funny that.

I'd seen it on the way to the pub. Friday was always pub night back then. Sandra called it our pub because it's the one where we met all those years ago. I've always hated the place and the night we met I was only there because the barman up the road had stopped serving me. But I thought it held great sentimental value to Sandra, the way things like that often do with women, so I pretended to like it. The problem with pretending, of course, is that there's never a good time to come clean without drawing attention to what else you might be faking, so 20 years later I was still there suffering in silence. Turns out of course that Sandra hated the place as much as me. We'd both been sitting there miserable all that time, me gazing into my pint glass like it was my own soul sloshing about in there and her twittering on about nothing in an attempt to disguise the silence between us that was heavier than the oak table we rested our elbows on. Anyway, by the time I got there that night I was in some state. I couldn't tell Sandra though. What could I say? I saw a bird getting killed. Big deal. So I just kept my thoughts to myself.

I've always had thoughts. You know – black thoughts. I'm a big worrier and have been as far back as I can remember. I suppose the worries I had as a boy seem pretty tame now but to the seven-year-old me they were as dark as they got and I carried them around like secret sacks of tar. Getting my homework jotter stolen in the middle of the night was my big fear. I'd be up and down the stairs all night, counting each one as I went, always holding my breath on stair number 13. Up, down, down, up. Breathe in, exhale. My mum thought I was a right weirdo. You'll die if you worry, you'll die if you don't, so why worry at all? That's what she used to say. I suppose it's sound advice up to a point – that point usually being when the thing you've been worrying about actually happens. Or when something happens, something that you haven't even got round to worrying about yet because your worries are backed up like cars on the Kingston Bridge at rush hour. That's the worst. When a fear you didn't even realise you had, is realised.

When that happens you have to deal with things backwards. The bad thing happens and then you realise that deep down you probably always feared it might but you hadn't got round to preparing yourself. Usually the fear comes first, you know? And you hope that by worrying about it a lot you might stop it happening. It's a weird, *a watched pot never boils* kind of logic but it gives you a little control over the situation. Well that's how it works for me. So those backed-up fears are the worst. They take you by surprise and that's enough to mess with any man's head if you ask me.

I'd just started taking my first sticky steps under the bridge when the wee guy flew down to see me. And I'm not just saying that now for dramatic effect. It hovered above the road staring at me and I stared right back. I saw the red car speeding towards it but thought it would be okay. Pigeons are quite dramatic. Always leave it till the last minute before they fly away. That's what I thought would happen this time but then I heard a noise like a crisp packet being popped as the car sped past.

They're not stupid, you know. Pigeons, I mean. They can store at least 300 objects or images in their minds indefinitely. At least and indefinitely. I saw that on the Discovery Channel years ago. That's what I was thinking about when I saw the wee guy hobbling towards me, blood trickling down his chest. How many of the 300 or so images in his head were of his fellow pigeons being squashed under that very bridge? Plenty, I'd guess. But it made no difference. Everyone knows they are going to die. It's not like you can hope it's never going to happen, like you can with a bee sting or getting trapped in a lift. But we all go through life like we have no expiration date. Why is that?

Anyway, I lifted him off the road. Me. The guy who

washes his hands ten times before dinner. I climbed over the barrier and cupped him in my hands, blood spilling everywhere. But he wasn't for being handled. He used the little life he had left to try and release himself, so I put him down before I dropped him. He took ten slow steps, leaving little red prints behind and disappeared inside a bush. That's where I had to leave him. Amongst all the empty beer cans, plastic bags and other shit that's been dumped there. That made me feel bad. Really terrible. But I had used up too much time already and I had to be at the bar for 17:58. It was an unspoken rule that I got there first. So I had no choice but to make my way to the pub, praying there was soap in the gents.

Pigeons mate for life, you know. Together forever 'unless forcibly separated'. Says so in *Pigeons for Everyone*, the book Sandra bought me. It doesn't say what happens after that – whether they hook up with another pigeon and try and forget about the old one or whether, like swans, they stay true to their loved one until death, mourning in solitude for years before their number's finally up.

I'd been mourning in solitude for almost 20 years by the night I saw the pigeon. The days were spent trying to distract myself with work, the evenings with drink. Then I'd lie awake all night trying to undo the past, get back to the point where it could all have been okay. The point where I'd made Jo stay at home and I'd driven to the shop instead. When I did finally drift off I'd be woken by nightmares where I'd hear Jo screaming for me. Every night for almost 20 years. I'd been with Sandra all that time but I was never really *with* her, you know? Not properly. That's why I'd never married her. It hadn't even occurred to me to ask. It would have felt like I was being unfaithful to Jo. My swan.

She died three days before our first wedding anniversary and three months before our baby was due. We'd chosen Sophie for a girl and I suggested Daniel for a boy but Jo said there was no need for boys' names, that she just had a feeling.

I buried them together. Josephine and Sophie.

Jo's family hated me. Thought I got over it too quickly, what with Sandra and everything. They said I'd just forgotten about Jo. That I'd never even loved her. Can you believe that?

That I'd never even loved her

Before the pigeon, if I let myself think about her — actually
dwell on it for more than a half second, I could feel myself
folding. And I knew that if I kept thinking, thinking about
what we had and were going to have, I would fold in on
myself completely and disappear. I truly thought that's what
would happen. That's impossible, isn't it? To fold in on
yourself. To disappear. But it was impossible for me to
believe that I'd lost the love of my life and my baby girl. You
see what I mean? All bets were off and I wasn't taking any
chances.

Do you think there can be thoughts without a thinker?
Sounds daft, doesn't it? But I had thoughts. I knew they were
there and I made a point of not thinking them. They were
different to my other thoughts. Take my job, for example — I
worry all the time that I'm going to lose it. They're laying
folk off all the time and it's probably going to be me soon.
That's a scary thought, isn't it? One I don't like to think
about if I can help it but it's my thought so I inevitably do
find myself thinking about it a lot more than I'd like to. The
ones about Jo and Sophie were different. It's like someone
had put them there without my permission. They existed
independently of me and I did everything I could to ignore
the fact they were there. And that was just the thoughts, not
what they were about. They were like boxes. Unopened
boxes in my head. I knew the boxes being there was bad
enough but the thought of lifting the lids and looking inside?
That just wasn't going to happen. It couldn't. That's how I
ended up with Sandra so soon. She was as good a distraction
as any and so long as I was answering her questions, I didn't
have time to ask mine.

Anyway, the pigeon. It suddenly became clear to me
and I knew what I had to do. I probably interrupted Sandra's
usual one-woman Q & A sessions when I made my
announcement but I'm not sure. I'd been sitting in that pub
for an hour and not said more than 'salt and vinegar.'

'I'm going to knock down the shed and build a doocot,'
I said. 'I'm going to keep pigeons.'

The idea was as much of a surprise to me as it obviously
was to Sandra, who for the first time in a long time was
speechless. Her face seemed the same as always. Then she

started. Took a mouthful of vodka, followed by a mouthful of air, and started. Hands poised like she was about to do a double karate chop.

'This is going to be the bowling club all over again, isn't it?' She'd wanted to say this for a while, I could tell. 'Remember? You bought the stuff – the shoes and the suit and the balls, you know, the ones you took about 2 hours feeling in the shop to make sure they were just right and then you went to the club twice, decided they were all arseholes and you just shoved all the stuff in the shed and forgot about it?'

She lowered her karate hands then picked up her vodka, downed what was left and slammed the glass down. Then she picked it back up, tipped the icy dregs into her mouth and slammed it down again. Leaning across the table so that her face was as close to mine as she could get, she crunched the ice so hard I could feel it in my teeth. I have very sensitive teeth. Sandra knows this.

'And about the shed,' she snapped. 'What you planning to do with all the crap inside it? The stuff you've crammed in there and forgotten about? What about that? I can't believe we're even having this discussion. You fucking hate pigeons! You moan about them every Friday! And now you want to build a home for them? Give them an open invitation to shit all over our garden? Sorry, *your* garden. Touch them? Did you think of that? You'll have to touch them, you know. And clean out their shitty loft day in day out. These aren't bowling balls we're talking about. You can't just shove pigeons in the shed when you get bored of them. Like you do with everything else. I'm surprised I'm not in the fucking shed.'

Then she did that thing annoying people do when they pretend to remember something really obvious – you know, when they hit themselves on the head with the palm of their hand. She did that. She does that a lot.

'Oh, but you're knocking the shed down. I forgot. So there goes that option.' She moved her face away from mine and pressed her back against the seat, arms folded, legs crossed.

'Did I moan about the pigeons once tonight?' I asked.

I leaned forward and tried to take her hands but they were still tucked away, one under each breast. So I leaned back and folded mine too. That made Sandra unfold hers. Just like I knew it would.

She laughed without smiling. 'You've not said anything tonight. So I've been sitting here trying to talk enough for the both of us as usual.'

She shook her empty glass at me.

When I got back from the bar she still looked mad and I realised I was going to have to tell her about the pigeon if I wanted her to understand. So I took a deep breath and suggested we walk home.

'But we always get a taxi.'

'I know we do, I said. 'But a change is good now and then. I think we need a change. Anyway, the walk will do us good. You always say you need to get more exercise.'

I offered her some of my crisps and she took a handful.

'Plus,' I said. 'There's something I want to show you.'

She rolled her eyes and let her mouth hang open. I could see mushed-up cheese and onion crisps stuck in her back teeth.

'Show me what?' she said. 'Why can't you just tell me? Although I can't imagine what you could say that would make *you* wanting to keep pigeons any less ridiculous.'

'Just do this for me. Please.'

She looked worried when I said that. When I still didn't go mad. She looked at me for a few seconds like she was trying to figure out where she knew me from.

'Okay, fine,' she said. 'We'll walk.'

'Thanks,' I said, letting out a sigh. I'd been holding my breath without realising it.

I'd prepared myself for it being dead but not gone. I started pulling out bits of rubbish from the hawthorn bush with my thumb and forefinger, placing it on the pavement beside me. Pretty soon I was crouched down next to a row of cans, a plastic bag and a Snickers wrapper. Sandra was standing just inside the bridge and saying nothing. I could hear her blowing on her chips and cheese. I'd been relying on the pigeon to really sell my idea to her, to help her understand. And now it was gone. And as far as Sandra was concerned, so was I. I didn't even like putting the rubbish out at home. And here I was, rummaging around amongst other peoples', looking for a dead bird.

'He was right here,' I said, using my clean hand to rub

my head. The way people do when they've lost their car keys.
I pointed towards the middle of the bush. 'Right there.'

Sandra put her carton of chips down at the bridge
entrance. On top of all that pigeon shit. I remember thinking
I wouldn't be able to hold her hand on the way home if
she picked it up again.

'I believe you,' she said, crouching down and rubbing
my back. 'Maybe a cat got to it or something.' She waited a
few seconds then gave my back a final pat and stood up.

I'm ashamed to say I started to cry at this point. Right
there by the side of the road. I'd never even thought of that.
That a cat could have ripped the little guy apart. I let Sandra
help me up. I was sobbing. Proper loud sobs. Neither of us
said anything for a minute or two, not that I could have and
Sandra, well, she didn't know what to say. But once we got
out the other side of the bridge I'd pulled myself together
enough to try and speak. I took a deep breath but Sandra got
in there first.

'I'll help you clear out the shed in the morning,' she
whispered.

We walked the rest of the way home in silence. But it
was a good silence. And that night, instead of staying up
drinking cans in front of the Discovery Channel as usual,
praying for sleep to come and save me from my thoughts, I
went to bed at the same time as Sandra. I wanted to be fresh
for the morning. The shed was crammed with stuff and it
was going to be some task trying to decide what to keep and
what to chuck.

Sandra always reads for a while to help her drift off so
I thought I'd try doing the same. She had a pile of library
books by the bed, all written by the same woman. The kind
of stuff Jo hated, I thought. Jo liked to read the Classics and
was always trying to get me onto them. She said I should
open my mind. I tried once, just to humour her. *Great
Expectations* by Charles Dickens. Took the guy ten pages to
finish a sentence. Not that I lasted ten pages. I didn't think
Over the Rainbow could be any worse, so I picked it up and
settled down under the covers. Sandra laughed when she
came in with her mug of hot chocolate and a copy of
Woman's Own and saw me all tucked up reading her book.
Said she didn't think I'd like it. And she was right. It was a
pile of crap – even worse than Dickens I think. I didn't say

any of this to Sandra though. She was going to see all Jo's books in the shed and I didn't want to her to think anything, you know? Like I thought she was less intelligent than Jo or something. She is less intelligent than Jo was but I don't think that matters. I'm not the brightest myself and I don't know how I ever ended up with a girl like Jo in the first place.

As I switched off my lamp, Sandra told me her books were due back at the library the next day.

'Maybe I could look for a manual to give you a few tips about stuff,' she said casually.

I don't think she wanted to mention the word pigeon in case that set me off again. It was a nice gesture. It's at times like that I feel lucky to have Sandra. I turned my pillow over to the cold side and as I lay there it suddenly dawned on me that for the first time in 20 years I'd had a thought about Jo. More than one. And I'd done it without falling apart. In fact I'd enjoyed the memories of her and those boring Classics.

Sandra says I fell asleep with a smile on my face that night. And do you know something? For the first time in years I slept straight through.

Dorothy Baird

DAWN AT BENARES

Darkness. A drumming of women
slapping and whacking
dirt from clothes. Knee deep
in the Ganges, suds floating
on the black water like flowers.
There is no sign. No movement
of the earth that asks for change

but change is written on the river
and somehow the almost light
floats in: that grey-blue time we give
no name as if we favour the gloaming dusk,
the twilight, the crepuscule,
when all promises are rescinded
and we are comfortable in regret

and not this eastern moment
when the sun begins to rise
over the smudged line above the scrub
in its veils of gauze
and we fall away
like smoke, like water, like thought
into this slow power of movement.

David Betteridge

FOX AND STARS

A November night;
no clouds; stars far beyond counting;
a crescent moon, oddly angled
as if laid back in hammocked ease;
trees, denuded almost, intricate in outline,
heaving in a chill wind;
frost on fallen leaves, brittle, breaking;
a pond, cement-contained, some way removed
from traffic's noise; no neon glare.

A short-cut home...

There, just out of reach, at rest,
with plumage fluffed, a fleet of swans!
Quietly, they bob. I stop,
but suddenly, with whummeling of wings
and thrash of feet, as one, they take to flight.
Not me, the cause,
but the red inruption of a fox. Now,
a seeming statue, long of leg,
brazenly he stands, aimed forward
from his cream-tipped brush to point of snout.
A boulder in the shallows is his plinth.

Intent, the two of us, fox and human, look:
we look upon the soaring white,
the silver of the moon, the stars beyond.
We look again, down low,
and see, cement-contained, their doubles
in the rippled shimmer at our feet.

Norman Bissell

READING RYOKAN IN THE RAIN

Reading Ryokan in the rain
a sad old man living halfway up a mountain
who wandered far then stayed put
and travelled further.

He wasn't after anything up there
content with his own company
he delighted in simple things
snow on the pines, writing poems.

Sure now and again he'd go down
and play with the kids all day
and drink sake with the boys
he was a monk after all

but mostly he liked just sitting
letting all of life flow through him
listening to the rain, watching the moon
reading old scrolls under a flickering lamp.

Ryokan means good-hearted
and you can see why
he's the guy who cut holes in his veranda
to let bamboo shoots grow tall.

He found love late in life
or maybe Teishin found him
it was her love that made sure
that he journeyed on.

In his poems you can touch Gogo-an
it's all so clear and crisp
you can hear the leaves fall around him
taste his salt tears.

At night he feels lonely
up there on his own
next day spring is fresh and green
this is all there is.

What is it about him that affects us so?
One robe one bowl
the simplicity of a life
pared down to the bone.

Now here I sit
listening to the sound of wind and sea
knowing his is the way
to drink deep of the water of life.

Eunice M. Buchanan

LAST RITES

I kent I wis ower late the meenit I turned the corner. She'd got the blinds drawn. I cuid hear her comin tae the door when I rang the bell an then the heavy key in the lock. I cuid tell by the soond o her feet. Draggin. No like her ava. Isa's aye been that nippy on her feet. She didna say onythin. Stuid there pluckin at the edges o her peeny an luikin duin.

'She's awa,' she says.

I went up tae her an we stuid there. No sayin onythin. Staunin there. Oor airms roon een anither. It's no a thing we go in for — in oor faimlie. I dinna ken hoo. We jist dinna. Isa had her heid in at the cruik o ma neck like a bairn needin comfortit.

'Are ye comin ben? Tae see her?'

I noddit.

It wis fell dark in the back bedroom. The curtains were closed. An in the bed wis oor mither. Aa worn awa an wastit — but she micht hae been asleep. Her haunds lay idle on the sheet an I reachit oot tae touch. I lookit up at Isa an she noddit.

'Speak tae her. If she's no richt awa she micht hear ye. That's whit the nurse said.'

I took her haund. It felt awfu strange — still warm, but idle. I had niver seen oor mither's haunds idle.

I tried tae think o somethin tae say but ma heid went blank. Isa noddit tae me, urgin me tae speak.

'Weel, Mum,' I wittert, 'I cam ower in the car tae — Weel, Mum — Roddy sends his love an —'

God Almichty, I thocht, here I am talkin tae somebody wi thir fuit on the lintel o Heaven or Hell — or the great everlasting eternity o Nothingness an I canna even say onythin! I tried shapin my mou intae the wirds, 'Mum, I love you.' But I cuidna. It wisna that I didna love her. It's jist no the kind o thing we say in oor faimlie.

An it micht upset her.

The room wis quiet. The pair o us sittin on aither side o the bed haudin her haunds. I lookit at oor mither's face — white, an tired oot, wi the shape o the cheekbones showin clear under the thin, gey near transparent skin. But nae mair pain. I lookit across at Isa. Same cheekbones. Same tiredness.

I shuid hae been here afore this.

'Come on, Sis,' says I, gettin tae my feet. 'That's her awa noo. Come through an *I'll* mak *you* a cup o tea for eence. An if ye're lucky ye micht even get somethin stronger.'

We sat for a bit wi a cup o tea at one haund an a nip o whisky at the ither.

There wir twa batteries sittin on the table. I lookit at Isa an raised an eyebroo.

'I took them oot o the clock,' she says. 'That's whit ye hae tae dae. Stop the clock.'

Isa sat there starin at the batteries. She sat back and lookit at me. 'That's whit I wantit tae dae,' she says, quietlike. 'Mum aye said she widna want tae gae on if she wis livin in an awfu state. We thocht aboot whit wey ye wid dae it — tae be maist comfortable.'

She took a wee sip oot o the gless an then held it up. 'I said that a big dram o whisky an then pu a plastic bag ower yer heid wid dae it. Whit a wey tae go!'

I smiled and noddit, no awfu shuir whit she wis gettin at.

She took anither moothfu. 'But I cuidna.' She shuik her heid. 'I used tae come in wi a plastic bag fu o messages efter anither nicht o oor mither screamin an screamin until the doctor got here wi his morphine. Sometimes she wid cry "Oh, my God, whit hae I done tae deserve this?" An she hadnae, she hadnae! I wid look at the plastic bag, an I wid luik at her. But I cuidna!'

She pokit at the batteries wi her finger. 'No aa clocks stop as easy.' An she stertit tae greet.

We sat thegither on the sofa an huggit an grat. An the hoose wis aa quiet an dark aboot us.

Syne Isa got tae her feet. 'I'll need tae phone the ithers an we'll need tae get the cheenie an the glesses oot. Dae we hae enough milk? What aboot the whisky?'

'Isa, sit doon a meenit,' says I. 'Here's a pen. Jist sit doon an get yer breith back. We'll mak a list on the back o this envelope an syne we can cross things aff. There's nae rush. Naebody's gaun onywhere.'

Suin we had the best blue an white cheenie oot, the

glesses polished, the cushions plumped and the room looked
aa richt. There wis a pictur o Mum on the mantelpiece in
her glad rags at the Club do. She wis smilin an raisin her
gless. A couple o year ago.

'That's the frock she got at the Co,' says Isa, 'an look at
her hair. She aye kept it that bonny. You're lucky. You've
got her hair. Look at me — flat as a bannock.'

'Richt,' says I. 'Awa ye go an get yer rollers switched
on. I'll see tae ye. At least it'll get ye sittin doon.'

I suin had her mair like hersel. I gied her a wee bit
back-combin an fluffed it up at the front. It wis jist fine.

'Come through an see yersel in the mirror. Is that okay?
Is that the wey ye want it?'

She noddit.

There we were stuid in front o the mirror on the
mantelpiece. Isa an me — an oor mither's pictur. It wis awfu
strange.

The same face — an no the same face — aa luikin at
een anither. An it wis as if oor mither wis there. Only she
wisna. It wis like we wis aa pairt o somethin — aa linkit
through an through een anither. I canna explain it. A lang
passage-wey o mirrors reflectin an reflectin Isa an me an
oor mither — an mair faces further back wi the same face,
an no the same face. They aa had that luik aboot them that
my mither used tae hae when she wis happy wi things the
wey they were. Jist a wee nod and smile tae say, 'Ye're daein
fine.'

An I thocht o the bairn in my wame. Anither face for
the mirrors.

I held oor mither's photo up tae face the mirror — an
she wis different. Ye ken hoo the twa sides o yer face are no
the same — an if ye get yer photos printit the wrang wey
roond ye ken it's no richt but ye dinna ken hoo no? Weel,
oor mither wis there aa richt — but no the same. I luikit at
my ain face in the mirror an it struck me then that I had
niver seen mysel as I really was — the wey ithers wuid see me
— the ither wey roon.

I luikit at her face in the photo an then in the mirror
an I suddenly thocht — whit wis she really like? I ken she wis
oor mither — an we cuidna hae had a better, but whit wis
she like? No as a mither or a grannie or somebody's next-
door neebour. But as a person — wi aa the thochts an desires

an guilts an aa thae things that yer heid has flittin in an oot aa the time. Wha wis she really?

An then I luikit at my ain face in the mirror an thocht I wisna awfu shuir aboot that een aither.

'I wis jist thinkin, Isa,' I says, 'if we dee an land up in heaven tae meet oor loved ones, as they say – we widna ken them.'

'How no?' says Isa.

'Weel, if it *is* heaven – oor mither's no gaun tae want tae be a white-haired auld wummin hirplin ower tae the Pearly Gates wi her zimmer. She wid be in her prime – a bonny lassie wi hair that's no ony colour that I've ever seen her wi.'

We sat starin intae the fire for a bit contemplatin the complexities o the hereafter.

'Come on, Isa,' says I, giein her anither wee hug, 'we'll jist sort the bedroom afore onybody gets here. I'll cheenge the watter in the flooers.'

When I cam intae the bedroom frae the kitchen Isa wis standin luikin doon at oor mither an shakkin her heid. 'She luiks terrible,' she says. 'Fowk are gaun tae be seein her an she looks jist terrible.'

The white spread covered the wee figure in the bed up tae her chin. Her bonny hair wis aa clappit in tae her hcid an draigelt luikin. We stuid starin at her.

'Awa ye go, Isa,' says I, rollin up ma sleeves, 'an switch on the rollers again – an bring me ma comb.'

Maoilios Caimbeul

TÈ GHEAL MO RÙIN

1.
Cuimhnichidh mi a-nochd, a thè gheal mo rùin,
far am biodh tu a' coiseachd
làithean fada geal air ais,
ri taobh Loch Shianta is suas dhan Choille Mhòir
's a-null ri taobh Loch nan Dùnan,
a' coiseachd a Chille Mhoire,
oir b' ann a' coiseachd a bhiodh sibh.

2.
Nuair a bha thu nad sheann aois
air an Acha Mhòr ann an Leòdhas
bhiodh tu bruidhinn mu Bhoilltir
is Flòdaigearraidh. Am measg nan truinnsearan
a bha air a' bhalla, 's tu air fàs dall,
bha na bruaichean 's na glaicean 's na lochan
's na daoine còire a bha air chall.
An aon rud a chitheadh tu ceart
mu dheireadh, b' e a' ghealach
agus sheasadh tu aig an uinneig
ga coimhead agus i làn.

3.
'S ann an seo far am biodh tu a' ruith 's a' leum
's tu nad nighinn bhig
tha cuimhne mar sgàile fo uachdar na tìre.
Seo far an robh a' bhàthach
's far am biodh sibh a' bleoghan na bà
's far an robh an sabhal 's stàball
's far an robh an seada an tacsa an taighe
leis na lìn is uidheam iasgaich
's far am biodh an t-iasg a' tiormachadh ris a' bhalla.

4.
Chì mi thu sna dealbhan anns na ficheadan
air sràid an Dùn Èideann còmhla ri banacharaid,
dreasa fhada ort agus currac
agus dealbh eile, air beulaibh an taigh-òsta sa Chaol,
tana is bòidheach is sibh air pòsadh
thu fhèin is m' athair
agus dealbh eile ann am Borgh Leòdhais,
thu cuairtichte le d' àl
agus anns gach dealbh tha thu caoin is caomh
is suairce mar bu dual dhut.

5.
Ged a bha thu dall fhèin,
bhiodh tu a' fighe. Mu dheireadh
dìreach stocainnean agus às dèidh do bhàis
shuidh mi a' coimhead orra, an tiùrr
stocainnean air an sgeilp. Sin mar a bha thu,
an còmhnaidh a' dèanamh do chàch
agus am Bìoball agus Crìosd
mar stocainn air do chridhe.

6.
An-diugh, tha na tha air fhàgail
air talamh dhiot anns an ùir ann an Crosbost.
Sìth gum biodh leat, a mhàthair gheal,
agus leis an fhear a tha rid thaobh.

MY PURE LOVE

1.
I will remember tonight, the bright one of my love,
where you would walk
long happy days ago,
beside the Sacred Loch and to the Big Wood,
or by Dunans Loch
on the road to Kilmuir.

2.
When you were old
in Achmore in Lewis
you would speak about Voilteir
and Flodigarry. Among the plates
on the wall, in your blindness,
there were the banks and hollows and lochs
and the kind people deceased.
The one thing you could see clearly
in the end was the moon
and you would stand at the window
looking at it in its fullness.

3.
And here where you would run and jump
when a little girl
memory is a shadow under the land.
Here is where the byre was
and where you would milk the cows
and where the barn and stable were
and the stance of the lean-to shed
with the nets and fishing equipment
and where the fish would dry against the wall.

4.
I see you in photos in the twenties
on a street in Edinburgh with a friend,
with a long dress and bonnet
and another photo in front of the hotel in Kyle,
slim and pretty, just married,
yourself and my father
and another photo in Borve, Lewis,
surrounded by your brood
and in every photo you are gentle and kind
and affable as was natural to you.

5.
Even though you were blind,
you would be knitting. At last
only stockings and after your death
I sat looking at them, the heap
of stockings on the shelf. That's how you were,
always doing for others
and the Bible and Christ
a stocking on your heart.

6.
Today, all that is left of you
on earth is in the ground in Crossbost.
Peace be with you, pure mother,
and with him by your side.

Jim Carruth

INTO THE BLUE

It was more than the pain of its recoil
the purple flourish of a shoulder bruise
that took several weeks to leave my body
more than their coarse laughter or tardy advice
that I should have held it firm like a man
or my worry throughout this rite of passage
my slow struggle to lift the double barrel
and its heavy weight to almost horizontal.

My father's success with it filled our pantry
but I never went hunting with him to the woods
instead I stood barefoot on a cold stone floor
and faced the lifeless works in his gallery
vermilion daubed across wing and breast
pheasant and mallard hung like roosting bats
lifeless hares also there flopped on a shelf
no longer themselves away from the field.

Now close to 70 he argues to keep his licence
as though the gun is a crucial part of him:
man-made like his plastic knee and hip
that prevent him from shooting on the hill.
Nobody else will use it; when he dies it will go.
On that day decades ago I was supposed
to knock an old soup can off the fence post
but winged a cloud and brought down the sky.

Alison Craig

THE DYNAMICS OF BALSA

You built model aeroplanes after school
in the disused light of your living room.
Balsa wood planed smooth, almost soft
beneath your thumb, its confection of dust
embracing the air. Your dad helped
with the glue, steady hand matching edge
to edge. Then there was fabric, paint,
and the weight in just the right place.
Such domestic aerodynamics.

You were ready then, radio control
in hand, running full tilt towards the
precipice, arm bow-tight like a javelin
thrower. Timing was key, the sweet point
of release, the perfect trajectory for
soaring, swooping, rolling like a
Battle of Britain pilot. You wide-eyed,
breath held, trailing years as I watched.

One day you rigged a camera into
the fuselage. It brought back to earth our
upturned faces, picked our expressions
from the wind.

Last week, Tuesday 10am,
you phoned me
from the airport.
This was for good,
you said. America.
You had a drink
in you. Flying
makes you nervous,
and your dad
isn't here to match
edge to edge.

I caught kisses tossed to the sun,
sparkling in your wake, spilling light
into your shrinking footprints.

John Cumming

DA NET

Böled anunder da broo o da banks, his knees draan up under his chin, da boy sat an watched da voe. I da rig abön him a collie made his daily inspection o rabbit höls. A hen dunter trötled tae her young-eens i da ebb, an across da voe, da single splesh o a divin tirrick set concentric rings in motion.

Still he sat, laith ta crack da moarnin's shell wi a rummle o keel on ebb-stanes. Aboot noo his midder wid be pletchin butt ta light da hob under da gruel pan, gantin an rexin as shu steered da spirtle.

Slowly he stöd tae his lent. Da collie caam dancin tae him, maakin play bows. Ignorin da dug he clambered doon da banks an lowsed da penter o da dinghy at lay noustet dere. Walkin tae da starn, he began ta haal her doon da beach tae da water. Eence shö wis flottin, he poled her inta deeper water, dan bent his back tae da oars. Da collie, resigned ta bein ignored, turned his attention tae da crang o a scorie i da ebb.

Comin tae da net fae da shore end, he began ta draa da dinghy alang da back, stoppin ta wash crabby lines, whaal blubs an da anterin green crab fae da mesh. Twice he stoppit ta unrivvel a fyshe, da first, a grey mullet, an dan a hoe, twistin an oagin in slow agony.

At da seaward end o da net, six corks wis doon. Reckin ower da gunnels, he drew da net tae him, an, rowwed i da lint, a muckle grey bird. On his knees da boy lowered his ketch tae da tilfers. Da haed an neck protruded fae da dark twine wund aroond da wings an feet.

Waary o da harpoon neb an glessy eye, slowly an deliberately, da boy began ta oonrivvel da bird. Twice, unlippened, da neb drew blood fae his broo an hands, afore he wedged da damp bundle under his oxter, an bent again tae his wark. Free, da bird wis surreal, unken, a shade fae some idder dimension. Da laegs wis ower fer eft ta support da weight; webbed feet subtle an clivver an da boady swack, busket i da colours o a winter sunset.

Boy an bird eyed een-annider in silence. Miles awa a diesel engine hammered inta life. Reckin, twa-handed, ower da gunnel he lowered da alien intae da water an, wi a

sprickle, hit wis gone, a shadow mergin wi da green o da
sea boddam.

*

*See my peerie bridder? His haed is fu o shite! He spends his
life in yun blödy dinghy or trailin ower da hill wi da collie.
Caam hame da idder day wi a mullet an a hoe fae his net.
Wha aets dat dirt?*

*Da teachers say he's clivver an der wantin him ta gaeng
ta Lerrick ta learn languages, dö Highers an dat. He could be
a doctor or a laawer or sometin, bit he'll no hear o it. See if
I hed his chances, does du tink I wid be wirkin in a fuckin
fyshe factory?*

*

*English – Neil is a quiet boy. His written work shows an
excellent grasp of the subject and a creative imagination, but
he should try to contribute more to discussion and debate.*

*Maths – Neil is a bright, able boy who has made
good progress, though he often seems distracted and tends to
daydream in class.*

*French – While Neil's written work shows good under-
standing, he lacks confidence in spoken French.*

*Art and Design – Neil is a difficult boy to teach. His
technical skills are exceptional, but he is defensive and
uncommunicative. If he could relax and enjoy his work more,
he has the capacity to excel.*

*History – Neil appears to have a genuine interest in this
subject. He has clearly done a great deal of background
reading, but fails to do the homework he has been set.*

*Sciences – Neil has made excellent progress. For a boy
who does no homework, he shows an outstanding grasp of the
subject. His understanding of Biology and Zoology is
exceptional.*

*Physical Education – Although he is fit and well
coordinated, Neil shows little interest in team sports and does
not relate well to his peer group.*

*

In his room, da boy lay apö da flör wi a book afore him. In
his hand he held a biro pen. He wis draain in a jotter, da
picter o a neesik, harbour porpoise, *Phocoena phocoena*.

I da keetchen, his midder an faeder sat facin een-annider ower da table, a caald tae pot atween dem. *Phemie, ah'm spokin tae him an better spoken, bit I can get nae sense oot o him. He'll no get dis chance again. He canna byde a bairn forever, an du kains as weel as I dö, der nae wark here bit sheep an salmon. Guid forgie me fur sayin dis, he's maybe clivver, bit der a want somewhaar.*

His midder sat, bitin her lower lip. Fur a while der wis silence atween dem. *Phemie, ah'm made me mind up, Ah'm sellin da boat. Ah'm pittin da dinghy i da paper. If he canna see sense noo, he'll maybe tank me fur it some day.*

Phemie stöd up. Her hand shook as shö gaddered lame fae da table an kerried hit tae da sink.

*

What I need, says da art teacher, stoppin ta draa braeth i da middle o his sentence, *is for you to pay special attention to the ellipses in your still-lifes. I set the cylindrical shapes there deliberately, to test your grasp of perspective. Treat the bottles and vases as cylinders and the apples as spheres. Remember to fill the page, we don't need acres of empty background.*

Brush i da water, dan i da pent, cobalt blue. Mix hit up, press hit till hit craems. Lodd da brush an start ta draa. Sit back. Draa fae da elbow, muckle movements. Pent runnin doon da page.

Sir! Louise Fullerton. *Kin I start again?*

Louise, you have just begun.

Bit Ah'm made an – I've done it wrong sir.

Louise, you will make many mistakes, but none that can't be remedied – persevere!

Bit Sir—

No. Come on now. Give it your best shot, and if you need help, just ask.

I need help.

Da teacher, his glesses prunk on da end o his nose, moves fae desk ta desk, offerin compliments, an encouragement; takkin da brush ta re-draa a line, add a colour. He stops at Neil Gölett's desk an stumsed, runs his hand trow his hair. On da page afore him is a weel advanced sketch o twa dunters, male an female, sweemin. Silence. Da teacher turns on da spot, noo scretchin his grizzled whiskers. He turns again ta Neil. *Neil, am I missing something here?* Silence. He tries again. *Neil, you're sitting in front of a still-life?*

Yis sir.

But you're painting eider ducks?

Yis sir.

Why, Neil?

Hesitation.

Hit cam intae me haed, an I wantit ta see if I could dö it sir.

But your exam, Neil, in two weeks time. Will the markers be impressed by ducks? Will you paint them in the style of Monet, or Cézanne?

Silence.

Deliberately he taks da dunter draain fae da desk an lays it on a table nearby, dan replaces it wi a clean sheet o paper.

Still-life Neil. Humour me. He stalks aff, hands ahent his back.

Neil sits, motionless, starin at da bottles an aipples; da white drapes; awaar o da een watchin him. Da bottles, tall, broon an green, caald an empty, kerryin no a wheef o da grape-scentet drink dey eence held. Da aipples, waxed an sheeny, wi nedder scab nor blemeesh.

Last Jön, hit wis, on da Broch Holm, i da middle o a frush o siggies. Da dyuke motionless, a broon fleckit ebbstane. Till suddenly, wi a flaachter o wings, shu liftet, laevin a skeet o musk-smellin shyte on da tree green aeggs. Whin he gaddered da doon fae aroond da aeggs, coverin dem fae da swabbies, hit wis warm, an da smell dark an plaesent.

Can we tidy up now? Louise Fullerton again.

Yes. Go ahead. Wash your brushes and palettes. Leave the sinks tidy.

Neil rises fae his desk an begins ta wash his brushes under da runnin tap.

Neil Goodlad, see me for detention at interval time.

*

James McKinlay, art teacher, drums his pencil on da desk. In front o him is a gaddery o books, pencils, papers, post-it notes, pens, draain pins an staplers. He looks up at da boy sittin afore him. Fair hair, cut short; a rash o fairntickles ower da nose, finger-nails chowed tae da queek. Da expression?

Resigned, patient even. A look at says, *Ah'm bön here afore.
Dis is aa I can lippen.*

McKinlay likket ta tink o himsel as an optimist, a carin
teacher. Bairns here wis, fur da maist pairt, bright an able.
Exam result wisna aathing, bit he hed management an
directors ta answer tae. Every noo an dan hoosomever, a
speecial bairn cam alang. A bairn wi a glig eye, a quick hand
an a hunger fur da subject. Whin he first met Neil his hert
quickened, dis shörely wis annider 'A' pass, annider recruit
fur da art schöls. Bit da boy wis akwaard, traan, an barely
spak. His wark hed nedder structure nor process. Der wis
nae denyin da skyill, bit i da comin exam dey wir lookin at
failure.

> *Neil, you're fifteen now?*
> Yis sir.
> *Tell me. Where do you see yourself in three years time?*
> Sir?
> *What would you like to do after you leave school?*
> Silence.
> *Neil, what do you like to do now?*

A clood passes ower da face, an dan – *I lik ta read* – *I
lik ta draa an pent* – *I lik*—

Da boy looks awa, blaet, colour risin in his face.

Defeated, da teacher rises fae da desk, walks ta his
bookshelves an, wirdless, hands a book tae da boy.

> *Neil, I give up. If you won't talk to me, I can't help you.
> You have a special talent, but if you're determined to go your
> own way, you must live with the consequences. Sit there and
> read till the bell goes.*

*Slave Ship Throwing Overboard the Dead and Dying;
Typhoon Coming On.* Neil gazes at da page. Sky an sea is a
swash o loord greys an blödy raedds. Da tree-mastet ship
rears i da backgrund, pale, already a ghost, da savagery o her
crew futile. I da boddam right o da picter, pale birds an
luminous fyshe gorge on da invisible jetsam. Da sonn,
glansin abön da horizon, stabs da hert. Da hale maelstrom
draas you in, spirals. Boat, birds an fyshe is immaterial, da
colour, da pent, da luminosity, brings an ache tae da hert.
Hits a reproduction in an art book, a picter, ten be forteen,
bit Neil can smell da pent, kaens da pain an ecstasy o da
dour, ill vaandet aald man at pentet dis in his studio
fortress.

*

Dew i da moarnin girse socks trow his trainers. Da laegs o
his jeans cling weet tae his cöts. Whin he comes tae da banks,
he laeves his bag upo da broo an soondlessly, aeses himsel
doon ower till he stands, a shadoo fornenst da mirror o da
sea. Fower peerie boats lie at moorins, teddered tae da banks
wi rops an pulleys. He walks alang tae whar da moorin rop
fae da smaaest o dem is secured tae a galvanised stanchion
driven i da stane pier, an lowsin da keeper rop, begins ta draa
her in towards him, hand ower hand. Da whilly nods her
haed an dan, gently, begins ta shorten da distance atween
dem, till shu lies within airms reach. Reckin in ower da boo,
he taks da penter an, wi twa half-hitches secures her tae da
pier, dan steps aboard. I da starn he lowses da screws at haad
da Yamaha ootboard tae da wharter, an dan, stiff laeged,
skurts hit tae da pier side. Wi a supreme effort, an a rummle
o wid on staen, he hents da engine tae da pier, follows hit
ashore an dan walks hit up da pier, clear o da high tide mark.
Twa mair trips empty da boat o da fuel tank an da unken
boat owner's fyshin gaer, afore he gadders his bag fae da
broo, lowses da penter an poles her awa fae da pier.

Settin himsel upo da fore taft, he slips da oars trow da
humlibunds an bends his back. Lightened, shu kerries clean
an aesy, as dey nudge trow tang an crabby lines ta clear da
shore.

An ooer later, da wastern horizon opens tae him as he
clears da Stiggies, da sonn is liftin ower da Bard, an da first
hansper is aesin fae his shooders. A sooth-wasterly swell,
kerried fae somewhar i da Caribbean, dandles da whilly.
Foula is a blue triangle whaar sky meets sea.

Lesley Dargie

THE DOCTOR SMOKED A PIPE

And I see the dog whining
In the corner where he kicked him
For snapping at his legs and then he said
The baby's dead and flustered
Filling out forms and phoning round
The dog whimpering and her
Screaming doorbells and policemen's
Boots going quiet
And smoke signals coming
From the pipe in his pocket

Derenz

FORBIDDEN STRANGERS

If only I could run forever, never be caught. My eyes struggle to keep pace with the ruts, tractor tyre clods, mole hills and their ankle-twisting subterranean runs. Rough cut stubble claws at the skin above my boots. I feel the pain of the split boughs woven through the hedgerow. I run and run. Almost giddy with the exertion, my lungs bring me down just as I reach the crest of the field.

The cottage seems small against the telegraph pole that stands mid-way between me and the enchanted hollow. And there's someone in the garden. Oh no, he's turning, the man will see me. I drop to the ground. Lie rigid, afraid the slightest movement will give me away. Then I twist my head to peek through the stubble, glimpse a view of that forbidden place. The man has turned away. Phew, he hasn't seen me. The smoke curl beckons from the chimney, I stand up tempted to cross the final stretch, speak to the stranger. I want to meet the airman, with the black face, who always waves. But the sting of the belt still pricks my memory. Anxious not to offend I turn and walk away, kicking the mole hills as I go.

I remember thinking, kick, if I don't look back, kick, the airman won't know that I've seen him, kick.

From the top of the tubular-steel gate, across the field from the cottage, I drop my hand to a lower bar and swing over. The ploughed field is tacky. I skirt along the ditch until I reach the old oak tree and squeeze between the hedge and its solid trunk. The wet clay on my boots greases the bulging roots and I scrabble to grip the gnarled bark. Grateful for the tree's girth, I find a safe spot before daring to crane, to peer between the hedge and security, and follow the smoke down from the chimney pots, to the moss-covered roof, to my forbidden friend in the garden.

Clouds shadow the sun, it is silly hiding here, I shiver, and watch as a fall of leaves snare on the hedge. I loosen the knot at my waist and struggle into my jacket. Off balance I fall into the hedge and a split bough gouges my arm. I yelp and scramble out, lick the wound and press my fingers over it until it seals.

The wind must have carried my voice: two children on the fence that bounds the cottage are pointing in my direction. I lean into the tree, watch as the airman joins them. He turns them off the fence and, after a glance my way, returns to work the garden. I think to myself, I am three fields from my house, out of sight really, and just one field from the cottage. No one would know.

I decide, I can offer to help. There can't be any harm in that. If things turn out not right I can run, and run, and no one will ever know. I follow the line of the furrow back to the tubular gate and clamber over. Stand tall. My mind and legs march me across the harvested landscape, towards the cottage.

I line my path by the telegraph pole, keeping its girth between the man and me, sure that I can't be seen. But there is no cover between the pole and the wooden fence. So I run; run straight at the fence, give myself no chance to be afraid. I pull myself up, my clothes part and a chill wind circles my tummy. The man keeps working.

He is digging potatoes. I watch his broad hands scoop them up and lower them into a wooden crate. He does not look up. But somehow, I know he knows I am there.

I need to speak, need someone to say hello.

'Can I help?' I say in a voice louder than I intend. He stops and looks up.

'Please. Let me help? I'm good at picking.'

He raises his hand. It is much whiter than I expect. He indicates for me to wait.

He twists round towards the cottage; I follow his line of vision and see a woman's face at the window. She looks at me and then at him and nods in response to his gesturing hands. He turns and strides towards me. To my joy he lifts me up and over the fence.

'Now,' he says, 'I've seen you running the fields but I don't know your name.'

'Ruthie, I'm Ruthie from the farm,' I say eagerly.

He looks me up and down and I stuff my vest and T-shirt back into my trousers.

'It's real good to meet you, Miss Ruthie,' he says and shakes my hand.

'Where are the others?' I say, looking round.

'My girls? They've gone in, they don't like cold and they don't like dirt.'

'But no dirt would mean no fields, and no plants,' I say, amazed that anyone could not like dirt.

The man laughs.

'Well we'd best work together. We'll need to be quick. The sun's going down. I'll dig. You put them in the crate.'

I prise the giant potatoes from clods of earth and rush to toss them into the crate.

'Now don't be pitching them. They're like apples, they bruise real easy.'

I didn't know that potatoes bruised but I wanted to please so I took great care.

'I like your cap,' I say. 'I've seen them through the wire at the base. Do all Americans wear them?'

'Why yes, most all,' he says, taking it off and fiddling with the back. 'There,' he says, and pulls it down to fit snugly on my head. I frown at the familiar waft of male sweat. But the heat trapped beneath my new cap is a comfort and allays any fears. He pulls his large parka-hood over his crew cut hair and returns to work. I watch, and proudly finger the peak of the soft green cap.

'Can I keep it?' I ask, as he positions the potato graip at the next shaw.

'We'll see.'

I clear the ground as fast as I can, scrabble through the earth to find the smallest potatoes. We are at the head of another row when a loud rap on the window calls him to the house. I don't look up. I want to keep working, stay in this garden with my new friend.

Out of the corner of my eye I catch his silhouette against the lit window. I hope they're not going to send me home. Hard as I try I cannot make out the words. So I lift his big fork and prod the stack of yellowing shaws. Instead of tidying the pile, the stems knot around the metal buds that blunt the prongs. I drop the handle and sit by the head of the fork and work to free them from the greenery. Before I know it, I'm being pulled to my feet and the fork, shaken free of shaws, is planted in the ground next to me.

'When are you meant to be home?'

'Seven o'clock,' I say, holding the shaft of the fork, and hoping the time is nowhere near seven.

'That's very late.'

'But not for me,' I say, afraid he will send me away.

When he says nothing but starts to tap his fingers against his mouth, I add, 'Dad works with tractor lights. I don't have to be in until him.'

The man looks at his watch, 'Come on then. We'll put things away and you can eat some with us.'

I help him load the crate on to a wheelbarrow and follow him round to a brick outhouse at the back of the cottage. It has boarded-up windows. The man leaves the barrow outside, struggles in with the crate. I follow, two steps behind, and marvel at the darkness and the waft of air as the crate hits the ground. But something falls, cloaks my head. I wrestle to free myself. Dust, smelling of mice and damp sacks, makes me choke. I stumble towards what I think is the door. Instead my face comes against the man's cold parka. I dodge sideways, trip and fall. I scream. And all Mum's warnings flood back.

'Whoa, whoa,' the man says, gripping both my shoulders; 'Shut your eyes. And count to ten.'

In a heap at his feet I do exactly what he says. At the count of five he lets go of one shoulder. By the count of seven I can hear and feel fragments falling. Something dragged, suddenly flaps behind me.

'Ten!' I shout, and leap up but can't see.

'Open up. Open your eyes, Miss Ruthie, now you'll see.'

I open my eyes. Gradually I see shapes, then lengths of what look like split coal bags, blackened sackcloth, hanging from crossbeams. The man was pulling them off and bundling them into the crate. The dust was thick and peppered with dried bird droppings.

'That should do it,' he says.

I brush my clothes and edge towards the entrance and the evening light.

'Right, you want a ride?' he says from behind me.

Without waiting for an answer, he swings me up and back on to his shoulders. He clamps my feet. I fix his fur-trimmed hood and find my balance. Together we feel our way in the semi-gloom along the path at the side of the cottage. I pull the hood back and press my lips close to his ear.

'Stop, stop,' I whisper and clasp his forehead. He stops.

'You want down?' he whispers.

'No, no, look,' and I point towards the telegraph pole;

'an owl, watch!' I barely breathe the words, every little muscle tense. I sink on my solid perch and mirror each tilt of the barn owl's face.

'We'll need to go in,' he whispers.

But the owl drifts down silently and as silently rises again. I am now high on the man's neck. I stare at the field mouse, so gracefully captured it never lets cry; and we watch the owl fly with its prize into the dark sky. We stay awhile, the night is so quiet, I gaze in the direction of the owl's flight and worry for the family of mice left behind then duck as a bat swoops close by.

As we reach the cottage door my ride leans forward and I drop softly to the ground. We use the bootjack to remove our muddy boots and enter into the warmth of the kitchen. The man's wife, holding a tray of cakes, snaps shut an oven door.

While I soak up the sweet smell of home baking, the man takes a knife from his pocket and frees the mud from the tread of my boots. He leaves his pair on newspaper by the door, and taking a floor cloth to mine, wipes them clean.

'You go on through,' the woman says; her white skin and English accent sounding strange against his American voice. I hear the girls in the next room, suddenly it doesn't seem such a good idea, not if they don't like dirt. So I stand where I am, close to the warmth of the Raeburn and hope they won't make me go through.

'Sam, take her jacket off, and that cap.'

I slip out of my jacket and Sam hangs it on a nail behind the door. I don't let go of the cap, but he makes no fuss. 'Come on, let's get those hands washed.'

His hand is warm. I feel proud holding the hand of this airman. He opens the door to the sitting room, the girls stare at me in silence.

'This is Miss Ruthie; and Miss Ruthie, this is Betsy-Anne and Mary-Lou.'

I think I say, hello, but I keep my face hidden under the peak of my cap.

Sam leads me from the sitting room, across worn flagstones into a dark soundless bathroom. A light clicks on and a latch drops behind me. He slips the bolt.

The stone floor feels frozen beneath my damp socks.

Sam turns on the tap. Water gushes into a spider-cracked basin and curls round and down the plug hole until steam billows and the stopper does its job. After testing the water he lifts me on to his slippered feet. He rubs soap on my hands, cupping them in his. He is gentle, cleans round my wound so that it doesn't open, and towels it dry. Then he wipes the mirror.

'Look at yourself,' he says; 'come, let me do your hair.'

'No.'

I stare in horror as the brush comes towards me. I clench my hands, creep backwards, my eyes flick from the bolted door to the steamed up window. Surely not Sam too.

He steps back.

'You do it,' he says quietly.

He steps further back and unbolts the door and I feel my heart slow. I don't take the brush; instead I raise my cap high enough to push the hair off my face and turn to Sam for approval.

'That's fine,' he says, raising the latch. 'Come, eat.'

The couch is smooth. I slide along it to the furthest corner from the girls. They are sitting on stools on a tufted hearthrug in front of the fire. While they tuck into peanut butter and jelly sandwiches I struggle to hide how I dislike the claggy paste which draws the moisture from my mouth.

'Here, have a root beer,' Sam says, and passes me a bottle of brown liquid. His girls were drinking it so I gave it a go. The unfamiliar flavour was okay and it helped me to finish my sandwich. The freshly baked slice of fudge brownie left a great taste in my mouth. I put the last mouthful to my lips.

'Oh my, Miss Ruthie!'

Sam stared at my hands.

I freeze, wonder if my last mouthful of cake is too big?

'We'll need to do something about those.'

Then I notice an expectation in his girls' eyes. I stuff in the last mouthful and drop my hand. Sam stands up reaches deep into his pocket and pulls out a penknife. He prises out a short blade and sits down.

'Come here,' he says and draws me towards him with his enveloping arm. Somehow it seems all right to slide along the couch, sit snug by his side. Betsy-Anne jumps up to sit at his other side.

'Me next, Pa.'

He takes first one hand and then the other, and with a relaxed firm hold, cleans the dirt from under my nails. I cuddle in. Suddenly everyone is laughing and chatting, and the fire glows. Sam's body so close to mine, so warm and so safe, my eyes sink.

I awaken to Sam's wife saying, 'Give her your new one, Sam. Buy another at the PX.'

Startled by the time, I look towards the window. It is pitch black outside. I jump up. I have half an hour, just half an hour to get home. Sam is close behind me. In the kitchen I fight with my boots while he holds out my jacket, warm from the pulley above the Raeburn.

'I'll need my cap, to walk you across the fields,' he says, hand outstretched.

I don't want to give it up, but I know it will only cause trouble in my house. I place it in his open hand, and dart through the kitchen door into the garden.

'Goodbye Ruthie, come again,' Sam's wife calls after me.

'I will, I will, thank you but I can't.' I call back, my head in a spin with thoughts of what will happen if they find out about my visit to the cottage.

I stare into a blank sky and follow the line of light from the open door and head towards the garden fence. My moon slips out from behind a cloud and Sam is there. He lifts me over the fence and vaults over behind me. We set off across the field.

I shudder at distant car lights moving up the farm drive. Sam stops, digs his hand into his parka pocket and pulls out a folded cap. 'Here, put this on.'

He adjusts it until it fits me snugly. He raises the collar on my jacket, then pulls the big furry hood over his capped head and walks on. I run after him and slip my hand into his, and he tucks my hand with his into his pocket. I feel his smile as he looks down into my upturned face. I push against him and together we tramp across the fields.

At the exit to the final field, before he sets foot on the drive, I stop him going any further. I take off the cap and hold it out to him.

'Go ahead. It's yours to keep,' he says.

Delighted but frightened, I lift my jacket and jumper as

one, and stuff the folded cap into the top of my trousers. I am sure I can hide it properly tomorrow. And in time I can pretend I was gifted it from one of the regular airmen at the base.

'I'll run alone from here, it'll be quicker.'

'Sure?' he says.

'Sure,' I mimic proudly. 'Do it all the time.'

He seems to understand, as if he too knows what is off bounds. I stand there with him in the darkness, I turn and look at the way we have come, it is all black, I turn back and a single light threatens over the farmyard. I want to go back with him, into the blackness and the comfort of the cottage.

My eyelid begins to twitch, my body shakes.

'Gee, are you okay? Here, I'll see you up the track, Miss Ruthie,' he says.

'No, no,' I say and turn away. 'You mustn't set foot on the drive. Promise?'

He laughs. He doesn't seem to be scared. Whatever.

'Okay, Miss Ruthie.' And he bent down and placed his hands on my shoulders. 'Now you be sure an' visit again,' he said.

I nodded.

'Now, straight home.'

I stand cracking my knuckles, the trees in the wood across the drive scary for the first time. I spin round on to the long drive. My heart pounds as my feet seek a safe rapid route along the potholed surface. I don't look back, in case there was someone in the woods and following me. I speed up but it seems to take forever before I see the dull light behind the farmhouse curtains.

Phew, Dad's tractor is turning into the barn. I stuff my hidden cap deeper into my trousers, and hope tonight, I'll get to bed without trouble.

I eat my supper in ritual silence and clear every scrap on my plate. My father disappears for a bath. My mother sends me to fetch my pyjamas and I race away from the chill of the kitchen, fly up the back stairs, dart across the landing to my bedroom, everywhere is cold; then down the front stairs to the blazing fire in the lounge where I spread my pyjamas along the fender.

The warmth loosens my tongue, and without thinking I present the back of my hands and my clean nails to mum.

'He did what?' she says clipping me fiercely across the head. 'You've been told not to go near that family. Where is this cap?'

I crouch where I am. My head tilted sideways away from the force of the blow.

'Where is it?' She shouts and raises her hand to hit me again.

I pull the cap out from under my jumper. Mum leans forward, snatches it from me, and flings it on the fire.

'I told your Dad. He should never have let those dreadful people rent that cottage. I knew there'd be trouble. I'll see to it they're moved on.'

I watch mesmerised as the blaze first wrinkles, then blackens the green fabric. Within seconds it turns my beautiful cap to white ash. For a moment it dances in the hot air, a piece catches on the soot at the back of the fire, and the rest disappears up the chimney.

'It's no good staring at the fire. Now bed, and there'll be no hot-water bottle for you, young lady.'

I want to tell my mother that Sam is kind, tell her how he washed my hands, carried me high on his shoulders, and how the girls had beautiful skins and black curly hair, and how we all laughed together.

Instead I gather my pyjamas, and creep out.

'Night,' I say from the safety of the door. And as I climb the stairs to my room, I fear I have done a terrible thing.

Andrew Elliott

MY AUNTIES

Back when the US economy
Was still rooting around in the dirt
For what all it would need to take hold
And become the great powerhouse we love today

My aunties were already growing old
In a little homestead in West Texas
Where they lived and very rarely saw anyone
Until with the passing of the years

If they hadn't had each other they'd've had no one.
For that (and the sky) they were grateful,
Thanking the Lord each night in their prayers
For having had the foresight to bless them with each other

And that was about it really. No late night chat shows
In those days, no B-52s on their way to wherever.
When they died they died together in bed
For that winter was brutal and a great wave of snow

Had swooped down from the north. After all what were
    they
But women. They had no rebuttal. When I found them —
Two skulls, one pillow — their quilt a kerfuffle of rats,
I could tell straight away how a grave was required.

The sun beat down hard on the head of a fellow. I thought,
The deeper I dig, the blacker the sky into which they'll be
    laid.
And when I brought them out tied in their sheet like swag,
It was indeed a great darkness had arisen. I was made.

Raymond Friel (b. 1963)

THE FLASK

Its emergence from some scullery depth
was a harbinger of short-lived summer,
like my father's clip-on shades or rolled sleeves,
my mother's top knotted at the navel
('What're you wearing that for?' he frowned one year,
and it was gone: a cloud over the sun).

At the beach it was lifted out and set down
replete with sweet brown drink, a sigh from the heart
as the cap came off in my mother's hand.
My father lit up, cupping the flame
for them both like a grown-up secret,
shooed us boys away to the water's edge.

When the high tide had toppled our towers,
the dregs were poured into sandy ground.
Then, the allurement of the interior:
all foil and reflection, fantastic light,
no trace at all of its turbid contents,
like looking into a soul, shriven and free.

Raymond Friel (b. 1974)

AN AMERICAN HITMAN IN GLASGOW

No one here to meet me at the airport terminal. A bad sign.
Unprofessional. I have an address but decide to wait. An
hour passes with me staring at a wall. Screw this. Walk out
into the afternoon grey and it's the same weather as New
York and almost makes me feel at home. Jump into a cab
and read out the address.

–Green Ock.

–Whit?

–Green Ock.

–Sorry pal, that disnae ring a bell. Sure you got off at
the right stop? Sounds like you shoulda stayed on until Hong
Kong.

–Are you trying to be funny?

–Whit's that? I cannae understand yer accent pal. You
Canadian?

–American.

–Aye I know, I was being funny. Gie's that piece of
paper.

I hand over the address through the mesh that separates
us. I see the cabbie's face, old, weak, lined with defeat and
too many cigarettes, and my own reflected in the mirror,
younger, uncreased, wolfen. We're barely the same species.
He laughs.

–Ya stupid cunt. *Greenock*. That's what yer wantin'. It's
one word.

–Did you just call me a cunt?

He motions to his ears as if he can't understand me
and starts the ignition, still chuckling to himself.

So this is Glasgow. Not much to look at, not that I see
anything as pretty soon we're on a freeway heading out of
town. The cabbie is still entertained by my mispronunciation
and as he drives I hear him telling his controller about my
mistake. The radio statics with laughter and while we drive I
hear the feedback as what seems like every cabbie in Glasgow
shares a laugh at my expense. I stare at his neck. How easy
it would be to jab the subtly sharpened key in my pocket
through the soft tissue below the skull and push upwards

56   *RAYMOND FRIEL (B. 1974)*

into the brain. I have done it before. Off the freeway now, must be getting close.

—Welcome to Green *Ock*, he says.

I don't respond. This is all part of it. Never show any emotion. Don't give them anything that lets them know they've touched you. Getting angry is a short cut to making a mistake and an assassin doesn't get second chances. We stop at traffic lights and another taxi pulls up. He rolls down his window and nods at the other driver.

—See this guy in the back? Picked him up from the airport, right, fuckin' asks tae go tae Green Ock!

—Eh?

—Aye, *Green Ock*. Said it like two separate words. The cunt thinks he's in China!

They both laugh. Jesus Fucking Christ. I make one mistake and it's made this bastard's fucking century. I'm getting this fucker's name and am paying him a visit after the job. Some unpaid overtime.

—You got a pen I could borrow?

—Sure pal.

He flings it through the hatch without taking his eyes off the road and it hits me in the cheek just under my eye. Well my friend, you have just played a part in signing your own death warrant. *Sean Wilson* is the name on the driver's ID card and *Sean Wilson* is going to pay. I write it down and lean forward to give the pen back to him as he hits the brakes and I fall forward and bang my head. He takes the pen, grinning broadly.

—Cheers.

I sit back. Will need to find a hardware store. Buy some razor wire and pliers. Perhaps a blow torch. Take a breath and think of Hassan-ibn-Sabbah, the Old Man of the Mountain, contemplating chess moves in his mountain fortress of Alamout. Though separated by centuries and thousands of miles I still feel a kinship to the man who gave birth to me, an assassin named after him, from *Hassan* — and not because his disciples smoked hashish, a mistake made by the sheep. It soothes me knowing that I am part of something greater than myself but unlike him not constrained by any doctrine. For those who deal in death the only religion they can have is a dead one. Look out of the window and take Greenock in. This place is worse than the little bit of

Glasgow I saw. If Detroit is New York without the glamour, Greenock is Detroit without the ... I can't think of anything. This place is just a shit-hole. Pass a group of kids playing with a dog, and then realise that they're not children, they're older, teenagers, just small, and they're not playing with the dog, they're trying to attach a firework to its tail. There's some commotion ahead and we slow down to wait for it to pass. Men dressed in black suits with bowler hats and white gloves, orange V's around their necks. The cabbie shakes his head and spits out of the window.

—What's the parade?

—The parade? Oh that ... it's a fuckin' gay rights thing.

Figures. Looking at the woman, a mix of the overweight and grotesquely ugly, they've got dyke written all over them. Never ceases to amaze me how far Hollywood gets from the truth when it comes to visions of lesbianism. Still, even for reality lesbians these ones are pretty bad, one passes picking her ass. Gay parades are either fun or angry and this is one is definitely angry. From the grim looks on the faces of the men Scotland must be a bad place to suck cocks. The meter continues to click as they pass and it's getting dark. We drive, the smell of a glue factory close by seeping through the windows. We stop again and the cabbie has another talk on the radio before turning to face me.

—Got a wee problem here pal. You're gonne ha' to beat it.

—Excuse me?

—That address you gied me doesnae exist. I've asked the lassie that's on tonight an' she hasnae got a clue. So, looks like it's the end of the road, cowboy.

—You implied you knew the address when I got in.

—Aye I know. An' I seen it was Greenock an' here we are. It's the actual street name but. I thought it was around here but I cannae see it an' I want to get hame. Your best bet is probably going into a pub and asking someone there.

—Well take me to a bar then.

—Which one?

—How the hell do I know?

—Okay okay. It's just they don't have any specialist bars in Greenock if that's what yer after.

—What is that supposed to mean?

He ignores me, not that it matters. We both know what

he was meaning. He is accusing me of being a homosexual. He is so fucking dead. We pull up outside a building that has metal bars protecting the windows. The doors of the cab stay locked until I pay him. I'm sure I'm being ripped off, £200 doesn't feel right, but I'll be getting it back later and smile at him as I get out, to his surprise. Turn my collar up and push the door open. I miss my gun. Not quite the stranger-in-town hush that descends in the saloons in the movies but enough looks in my direction to know that I'm being checked out. Let them, as if they could see anything I didn't want them to. There is a lingering smell of bleach in the air that isn't quite hiding something acrid underneath. No wonder everyone here is drunk. I move to the bar and a small man with thick glasses stares at me over the counter.

    —What d'you want?

    —Milk.

And this time the hush from the Westerns does descend. That was a mistake.

    —Whit?

    —Milk. Forget about it.

    —*You a pussy or summit?* I hear a woman's voice call from somewhere behind me, I ignore it, and the ensuing shrieks of laughter.

    —Do you take UHT? says the barman.

    —What's UHT?

    —Long life milk.

    —I said forget about it. I don't want anything to drink.

    —*Well get tae fuck then!* shouts the same woman who called me a pussy.

What is this bitch's problem? I put the piece of paper with the address on the bar.

    —Do you know where this is?

The barman glances down, chuckling to himself, but stops when he sees the writing on the paper. He looks up at me and smiles.

    —So you're the hitman eh? How are you finding Scotland?

I freeze but no one else in the bar seems to have heard him and I'm too stunned to answer.

    —Wee Billy was in earlier and mentioned that he'd got some professional help in fae America if you're wondering how I know.

He's waiting for me to confirm the statement, but I

don't. Can't. An old man stumbles into me as he leans over
the bar to get an ash tray.

—Watch what yer doin' James, that's a professional killer
you've just banged into, says the barman, winking at me.

—...I'm not a hitman, I don't know where you got that
from but I certainly am not a ... what was it you said? A
hitman?

—Aye, right you are.

He winks at me again while the old man places the ash
tray on the bar and drops a butt in it.

—It's nothing to be ashamed of, says the old man.

He winks at the barman and the barman winks back at
him and I'm caught in the crossfire. I shake my head. I will
need to kill him. Kill them. My identity must remain a secret.
Fuck. The old man hasn't even stubbed his cigarette out
properly and the smoke is choking me.

—Could you put that out properly?

—Sorry son.

He spits in the ash tray, missing the ember the first time
but getting it with black phlegm on the second attempt,
though some of it splashes out and hits my hand before I can
move it away.

—Don't kill me! says the old man, pretending to cower.

He laughs and the barman joins in followed by the rest
of the twenty or so people in the bar who must have been
listening in after all. Hassan-ibn-Sabbah did not have to
put up with this. Right. I need to firebomb this bar and
make sure nobody gets out. And the taxi driver. He's also
part of the problem. But first things first. I need to get out
of here.

—So where is it? The address, I say to the barman.

—It's quite tricky to get to if you've no been there before.

The old man takes the piece of paper with the address
on it from my hand.

—That's on my way. I'll take you if you buy me a fish
supper.

—How much is a fish supper?

—Three-no. A tenner.

—Deal.

Turn and walk to the door sensing all eyes on me. I flick
my collar up and make my face the mask I wear when I kill.
Somebody wolf-whistles.

Outside. Suck in the air and start coughing. I'm underneath
some sort of vent puking gritty smoke. But at least the first
piece of good luck, a gas canister is lying at the service hatch
and gives me an idea.

—Gies a second son. I need a slash, says the old man.

Perfect. While he staggers up an alleyway I take the
canister and position it at the vent. Open the valve and—

—Whit you dae'n wi ma fuckin' gas?

Something hits me on the back of the head (a shoe?)
and I drop the canister. A middle-aged woman with blood –
no not blood, lipstick – where her teeth should be grabs
the gas and picks up her shoe.

—Ya thievin' cunt.

—Miss, it's not what it appears. I will gladly buy that
canister from you.

—Do I look fuckin' stupit?

—I don't really know how to answer that question. Look,
I have money.

Show her the wallet. Get her in close enough and the
piano wire coiled in my sleeve will do the rest. But I need the
element of surprise to do it cleanly, she's got to approach
me.

—There's fuck all in there.

What? Check the wallet. Some bastard's robbed me.
Fuck. Somebody in the bar maybe? Fuck.

—What's wrong wi yer coupon? Ye gonna start greetin'?

This bitch is going to die, like everyone in the bar and
the taxi driver. Need to keep track, make sure I don't forget
anyone.

—I've got another wallet. Come here and I'll show you.

Money. It always works with women. Or men. But
women especially.

—Naw. You don't have any Buckie do you?

—What's Buckie?

She shrieks with laughter.

—Ya daft cunt.

—Leave him alone. He's wi me, shouts the old man
returning from the alley.

The grey tip of his penis is poking through the undone
buttons of his trousers and is angled my way. She sees his
cock and points at me, laughing even louder. I step in her
direction but the old man grabs my arm and drags me away.

I shake him off, wanting to silence the woman, needing to destroy the bar to keep my identity safe but realise that will have to be done after the job. It's time to move. He stops. We're at a fish and chip shop.

–Take me to the address first.

–This is the best one but. C'mon, it'll only take a minute.

–No–

He ignores me and enters. So do I. Even though the smell is enough to turn my stomach there is a queue.

–I'm not waiting. Do you want your money or don't you?

–Oh aye.

But he doesn't follow me as I head for the exit and instead I hear him approach the top of the queue.

–Gonnae let us in first 'cause I'm looking after that guy there, aye the hitman wee Billy was going on aboot.

You have got to be kidding. Turn and grab his arm but there's some wiry muscle underneath and he's able to hold me off.

–It's aw'right pal. Gies a minute, I'm being served.

Can feel the eyes watching me. Try to relax. Take a deep breath and block everything out. The old man nudges me.

–Ye wantin' tae share a sausage supper?

–No.

–See there's two sausages. We could huv one each and split the chips.

–No.

–So you're a hitman eh?

A young man's voice from the queue. Pretend the words weren't said.

–Cause ye dinnae look very tough. I reckon ma wee brother could knock fuck out of you, an' he's only seven.

Laughter and then another nudge from the old man.

–What about a pickled onion?

My body moves without my control and I lift him out of the shop and take my key out and hold it to his neck millimetres from the vein.

–Take me to the address or you die.

A second passes as first the surprise and then the fear registers before he nods and I let him go. He's frightened and backs off pathetically. Submissively.

—There's no need to lose the place, big man. I'm taking you there right now.

We walk in silence. He will have to be killed. As will everyone in the fish and chip shop. The old man is ahead of me, mumbling to himself, getting worked up. No point getting this far and blowing it.

—Take it easy, old timer.

—I'm 38 fur fucksake. Fuckin' old timer ma arse.

—...Sorry.

—Wank.

He stops and points at a house at the end of a street with no lights.

—That's where yer goin'.

—Okay—

He punches me in the face and runs off, disappearing in seconds. My nose is bleeding. Initial urge is to go after him but I'd never find him in the dark. But I will see him again, I know it. The world is a lot smaller than you think. A day, a year, whenever. It will happen even if it takes a lifetime. Mop up the blood coming from my nose with the sleeve of my suit and put on my game face. I have a job to do. I am a professional. And whoever this Wee Billy is will have to be dealt with for shooting his mouth off. No wonder they had to call me in. Everyone in this country is a retard. Lots of boarded-up windows. A normal person would be frightened walking down this road. But not me. At the door. Ring the bell.

—Ya fuckin' arsehole!

It's the old guy at the end of the street, come back to gloat.

—How'd you like the skelp in the mooth?

What's his fucking problem?

—Aye, that's what you get, that's what you get if you mess wi' the big boys!

He's too far away to reach and anyway, I've already rung the bell. Try to blank him out.

—You're the fuckin' old yin by the way! Check yer gear! Yer wearing a de-mob suit!

I need to deal with this before the door opens.

—Look, just get lost. I'm not talking to you anymore.

—Shitebag!

But at least he turns to leave. I hear the rustle of keys

and the door opens a crack. The only part of the face visible
is covered in acne.

—Who the fuck are you?

—Step aside kid, I'm the cleane-AH!

A stone hits me on the back of the leg and I fall to one
knee. That old bastard! He's fuckin' dead! Top of the list.
Forget about the taxi driver, the people in the bar and the
chipshop, the woman with the gas canister. He's the one
who will pay. The spots haven't moved, still waiting for an
answer. Another stone skips off the pavement but this time
misses.

—Just let me in for Christ's sake!

—I cannae let you in if I don't know who the fuck you
are.

—I'm the Yank!

—Right. Gies a sec.

He turns and shouts to someone I can't see.

—There's an American here wantin' in. Calls himself
The Wank.

Laughter and then,

—Let the cunt in.

I step inside. Three men and the boy that answered the
door. Two of them have their shirts off, and while I'm used
to seeing it in LA, where even the drug dealers work out, this
pair have nothing to show off. Not that they're fat, the
opposite, so thin and white their ribs are showing. One of
them absently kneads a boil on his shoulder while the other
points at the kid.

—Pay no attention to that wee shite. He disnae know that
wank means summit else where you're fae. It's just funny
cause over here it means fiddlin' wi yersel. Not something
any cunt would want tae call himsel.

I let it pass. A new feeling, no not new, just something
I've not felt for years. I want to cry. Oh Christ.

—Take a seat, pal, and we'll go over the particulars.

I slump and sniff. His eyes narrow.

—You are the fuckin' hitman in't you?

—Yeah.

—Good. Well I hope you got a sleep on the plane, 'cause
you're gonnae be busy. There's about fifty cunts that need
doin'.

—No. That wasn't the deal. I was contracted for one job.

—Look pal, we're no payin' you three grand for just one.

—It was five. Five grand. Plus expenses.

He looks at the other guy who shrugs.

—We can get aw that sorted later. I fuckin' hate talkin' about money. C'mon, you wantin' a drink?

The memory of the bar is too close to be repeated so I nod. He hands me a bottle.

—Buckie, I bet you don't get that in the Bronx.

He's staring at me, waiting for me to drink, so I do, and even though I keep my lips closed some of the syrupy mixture gets through.

—Fuckin' good innit?

—Sure.

Screw this. I take a full drink and gulp it down.

—That's the game ma man!

I almost cough but hold it in. Now then, to business.

—Where's my gun?

—Eh?

—Not *my* gun. *The* gun. The item I requested for the job.

—You're holdin' it.

—What?

—Aye, wee bit of a problem gettin' the shooter but they're for shiters anyway. Just use the bottle after you've finished wi it.

—Let me get this straight. You want me to kill fifty people with an empty bottle?

—Aye.

Sometimes it's best not to say anything. So I don't. But a thought is bubbling deep inside that terrifies me.

—If you preferred a blade we could do that. Or extra bottles. Probably no Buckie ones but. You'd probably feel more at home wi empty Coke ones than Irn Bru eh?

His voice continues but I'm not listening anymore. Did the plane explode ? A suicide bomber or unexpected technical hitch? Killed before I realised it? Am I in a thousand pieces falling into the sea and caught on the tide of the Atlantic? Am I dead? Am I? Because it would certainly explain today. And if I'm dead then this is hell and as soon as I think it it comes out of my mouth, no circuit breaker between my brain and vocal chords.

—Is this hell?

They all laugh. It is.

–Naw pal. It's Greenock.

They laugh some more and so do I. I take another drink and notice a picture on the wall of what must be last year's gay parade and can't help myself.

–Jesus Christ, is everyone in this country a fag?

They stop laughing.

–Whit's that yer sayin'?

I point at the picture on the wall, the orange sashes and white gloves, more serial killer than screaming homosexual but it's no surprise that in Scotland not even the faggots know how to dress.

–The gay parade. No wonder they suck cocks 'cause they sure as hell couldn't get any pussy.

–You calling the Orange Lodge a bunch of poofs?

–Why is called the orange lodge? Shouldn't it be the pink lodge?

What happened next happened so quickly that it's only now, in the boot of a moving car with what feels like a broken jaw and blood leaking from my anus that I can even attempt to piece together the order of events that got me here. As soon as I said 'pink lodge' there was a look exchanged between the three men and a bottle hit me on the side of the head and I fell to the floor. Blurriness next as they kicked me but not too bad, and I was close to getting up when I heard the words—

–*Put the fuckin' heel in!*

And then nothing. Until now. God only knows why my anus is bleeding. Only in Scotland would the homosexuals be psychotic. But if this is meant to make me change my ways, re-think my life and decide to spend my time helping the poor or volunteering in an animal sanctuary, fate is sadly mistaken. I am going to get better and then kill everyone on the planet. I smile and hear the bones rubbing together. Smiling's out for a while, perhaps for good. The car stops and I wait for the shots. Instead the boot opens and I'm flung onto the road and they leave me. I'm in a strange country in the middle of nowhere with no money, a broken jaw and an anus that is beginning to gush but at least I'm alive. I'm alive ... Oh shit, they're not leaving, they're reversing—

Graham Fulton

DALI RAGE

At the foot of *Christ of Saint John of the Cross*
a man in a Seventies Soviet top
with CCCP in big white type
goes mad as he tries to photograph
the immaculate oil on his *Virgin* phone.

Excuse me he tuts to pensioner gangs
who shuffle his arty field of fire.
Worshippers keep on barging across
with buggies, crisps and *Somerfield* bags.

He turns an atheist shade of red.
He feels as if he's about to burst.

A small boy with a Roman helmet
squeezes and weaves his way to the front,
determined to get a place
at the crucifixion, Jesus without a face,

hanging in sky above the sea.
Everyone loves a surrealist with taste.
Forgive them Sal, they know not what
they do. Messiahs bring out the worst.

Valerie Gillies

THE EYE WELL
for the painter Helen Parry Jones

Born blind in one eye, when your good one
was threatened, your mother upped and carried you
around the wells of Ireland: the wee girl
douking and dipping your head in pools
as if for apples.
                    At one overgrown place
she cleared away the grass and nettles
to wash your eyes in a pellucid spring.
It wept for you. And you peeped out
towards sky and trees recorded on the surface

with the eye-baby appearing in the centre,
your own diminutive reflection eye to eye
returning your long look. The wise water
kept getting clearer as you watched. Today

your good eye sees far more than most.

Merryn Glover

HER MOTHER'S SONGS

The village street is deserted. From the far end, where the bus stops, a girl walks up the pavement, weighed down with bags. On this autumn day she wears a thin floral dress, hiking boots and a nose ring. A gust of cold stirs the tangles of her sun-bleached hair and makes goosebumps rise on her skin. Brown and brazen as a native, Mother would have said. In one hand she carries a battered doctor's case and in the other three supermarket bags, bulging and awkward. On her back is a giant rucksack covered with badges. Wai Ki Ki Beach. Love. Tibet.

In the middle of the street she stops. The Atholl Arms is shuttered and quiet at 11am. Next door is the charity shop with knitted teddies and a row of dusty paperbacks in the front window. Next to that is Scissor-hands Hair Salon. The windows are fogged up and as the door swings open with a tinkle it breathes out a puff of steam and the figure of a woman. Her hair is coiffed and sprayed stiff like meringue.

On the other side of the street is the house. The pebble-dash walls have grey streaks running down from the corners of each window, as if the place had been weeping. Silent now, those window eyes sleep behind net curtains. The red door between them is faded to a tired pink, scratched and peeling. In the garden, brambles fill the flower beds, straggling out to the knee-deep grass and the clumps of weed.

The girl walks up the dirt path to the door and puts her bags down on the step, easing the heavy sack from her shoulders. The patch of sweat on her back feels suddenly cold. There is a doorbell but it makes no sound. She knocks. No answer. Knocks louder and there is a faint scuffle inside but then nothing.

'Hello?' She calls out, tentatively, then bangs on the door. Silence. 'Anyone home?' She bangs louder, pounding her fist this time, but only to hear the silence pushing back against her. Just the distant swish of a car on the by-pass road. Hoisting her bags, she walks down the side of the house. The curtains at one window are hanging in torn strips, like flypaper. A pane is broken. Round the back it looks like

the house has disgorged itself into the yard. An old couch
with springs thrusting up through the cushions sits under the
apple tree. A washing machine gapes with vacant mouth at
the back fence. Bits of wooden furniture lie across one
another, like bodies in a mass grave. Legs sticking out, table
tops split and lifting at the edges. Tangled amongst them is a
mess of household flotsam. Telephone books swollen with
rain, a child's clothes, stiffened blankets, a kettle. Beside the
shed a pile of cardboard boxes lies in a sliding heap, softened
and speckled with damp.

The girl looks back at the house. The sunroom porch
sags at one end and most of the glass is gone. Bindweed curls
into the room, strangling the clutter of pots, plastic bags
and shoes in its path. Inside the porch, on the back wall of
the house, the kitchen window is cloudy with grease.

She knows her mother is home.

Putting her bags on the sofa, she brushes her fingers
across the torn upholstery, remembering when its green and
gold flowers were new and how she'd hidden behind it and
cried. She checks the back. The hole is still there. The hole
she'd dug out with her fingers, a bit bigger each time till it
could hold her treasures. A pebble, a ribbon, a stolen
biscuit.

The porch door, when she tries it, is jammed against
something inside. She pushes and rattles then feels that rising
fury that makes her want to kick it down, but she checks
herself. She is not here to fight. She is here because Aggie at
Scissor-hands Hair Salon wrote, on a blue airform letter, that
she should come.

'Mother!' she calls out to the back wall. 'Mother! It's
Laura.'

The house gives away nothing. Not a twitch of curtain,
not a creak of board.

Laura goes back to the front door and tries it, knowing
full well it will be locked as it always was. As a child she had
wondered what a front door was for, since they never used
it. The milkman would be banging and there was Mother,
sitting at the table with her cup of tea and her biscuit, staring
steadfastly into the back garden. Not moving but to dip her
biscuit, bite it, sip her tea. Same went for the minister. And
the neighbours.

'If you're not careful, folks'll take over your life,' she

would say. Letters she ripped up and turfed into the fire.
'Keep yourself to yourself and don't let anybody tell you
what to do.'

Which is why Laura never went to school. Mother didn't
believe in it. Nor doctors and their meddling, or busy-body
church ladies with their plates of scones and beady eyes, or
complaining neighbours, or snooping social workers, or
bossy policemen. The lot of them could just go to hell.

There was another way in. Laura had finally discovered
it, when she was nine, as a way out. One night, when all the
doors and windows were shut fast and she was locked in
her room, she had noticed the rotting wood around her
window. She dug it away, quietly, slowly, over many nights
till she was finally able to lift down the pane – *carefully,
carefully* – and climb out.

That first night she didn't go far. Just out, barefoot, into
the empty street and down to the darkened windows of
McIntyre's shop where Mother used to take her for the
messages. It had been every day when she was tiny, and then
less and less, till Mother went on her own once a week while
Laura had to stay at home. Mother always said she was
sickening for something and she'd catch her death.

In the end, even Mother didn't go. Mr McIntyre had said
something and she was never going there again. Got a
delivery from the grocer's in the next village instead. First
week he tried to bring it all into the kitchen for her but
Mother was having none of that. From then on he left it on
the back step next to the jam jar where she put the money.

'Folks are that nosy,' she said. 'Keep your distance, Laura
Jane, and they won't touch you.'

Each night Laura crept a little further. Along to the play
park where she would whip down the slide in her nightie
and ride the swing almost high enough to kick the stars.
Then down the burn to a waterfall with a pool so cold it
made her gasp. Over the hills behind the village to startle
sheep and scratch her legs on gorse. And once, she went right
up to the high pass where she saw a big town in the valley
beyond, like a sea of lights. The next night she went down
into that sea and into the bright doors of a police station and
into the world.

Laura moves quietly now round the other side of the
house to her old bedroom window. It is boarded up. From

the inside. Rough planks are banged over every inch of that escape route, the wood splitting from the force of the nails.

Back on the sofa under the tree, she pulls out from the doctor's case the few things she took with her that night. A copy of *Just So Stories* with a gold elephant's head pressed into the hard navy cover. Her Peter Rabbit mug that Mother had given her twice a day filled with warm milk. A black and white photo of her as a baby with Mother and Father. It is slightly out of focus, but clear enough to see the wind blowing Father's hair into a cock's comb, and Mother clutching her hat with one hand and gripping Laura with the other. Clear enough to see his laughter and the lace on Laura's dress. 'Your Mother made that frock for you,' Mother would always say, proud, defiant, as if it proved something.

Father was more a belief than a memory. Laura's faith was in a man who'd been tender and funny, whittling little toys and riding her up on his shoulders. And one day, he would return – perhaps without a white horse or trumpet's cry – but certainly to take her with him to the place he had been preparing: Father's house with many rooms. How else could she explain him leaving her alone with Mother?

Mother, who had faith in nothing, god or man. Who gave her hand in marriage but not her heart. Who stacked up her grudges like the sheets in her linen press and polished every slight and snub and funny look like silver in her drawer. Father had tried to win her over, but she was not to be saved from her bitter disbelief in goodness. When he did not share her disdain for other folks, she included him in their number. His failure to mould his view to hers was, in her mind, final proof of the impossibility of love. Her only hope was a child she could make in her own image. Thus, once Laura was delivered, Father was of no further use.

He was too tall for their house, anyway, always banging his head on the lintels and cursing. He had to find a taller house to live in, Mother had explained when he disappeared. Then she pressed her lips together and never spoke of him again. There were many things of which she would not speak. Her own family. Where she'd come from. Why folks were Not To Be Trusted.

The last thing Laura takes from her black bag is her wooden recorder. Mother had taught her. It was the first lesson of each day's 'home-schooling'. Mother had read an article about this new-fangled practice and seized on the idea like a life-ring to a drowning man. Oh, the relief, the triumph: Laura needed no one else but her.

From that moment, the child was spared the dark influences of teachers and preachers, librarians and travelling players. Safe from the risks of walks, bicycles and picnics. Free from the intrusions of dinner guests, birthday parties, friends.

Mother had no sheet music, so taught by memory, tapping time with a wooden spoon on the table. *Twinkle Twinkle Little Star. Row Row Row Your Boat. Frère Jaques.* Each one note-perfect before the next could begin. *How I wonder what you are.* Over and over again. *Merrily, merrily, merrily, merrily.* Till fingers were sore and back stiff from good posture. *Are you sleeping? Are you sleeping?* Till Mother would grunt her satisfaction and they could begin maths with the button box. *Life is but a dream.*

The sky above Laura is bruised black and grey. As she puts the recorder to her lips, a soft, barely-there rain begins to fall. A silent crying, not daring to weep. It falls without sound on the cardboard boxes and the broken furniture, the little girl's dresses strewn across the grass, the toaster, the unopened mail.

Laura plays. She's learnt many tunes since leaving home. *The Skye Boat Song, Cavatina*, Beethoven's *Ode to Joy*. She even spent a year travelling with a Baroque recorder quartet around Australia. But now, after getting Aggie's letter – because Laura always reads her mail – she has come back. And for this occasion she plays her mother's songs. Sitting on the exploded sofa under the apple tree in the rain. *Baa Baa Black Sheep. Have You Ever Seen a Lassie. Three Blind Mice.*

Paul Gorman

THE FIREWALL

It was only the delivery man. The buzz of the entryphone
hung in the air. Martin shut and locked the door while the
courier still stood on the doorstep. He peeled the shrink-
wrapping from the small cardboard box, feeling like a child
on Christmas morning.

Away from its bed of polystyrene the neat plastic device,
in sleek grey and black, was so small – about the size of a
credit card holder – that Martin felt disappointed. He read
with a mixture of scepticism and anticipation the claims
made by the manufacturer. Surely it couldn't be *that* good?

*The Personal Firewall. Why stop at just safeguarding your PC?
You are far more valuable! Our handy, easy-to-use device offers
guaranteed protection from unwanted attention. Soothe away
the hassles of modern life. Available in a variety of colours.*

He examined the unit. A push-button turned it on and
off, and a small slider changed the settings from 1 to 5.
Additionally, there was a *stealth* mode which offered, the
instructions claimed, supreme concealment but also sucked
the batteries dry. He slipped the device into his pocket, but
as he was still at home, there was no way to test it. He
nudged it up a few notches and went to catch a bus into
town.

The village was quiet. What few people were about
ignored him. When a bus appeared at the road-end, he
stepped from the shelter to hail it. The bus driver didn't even
slow down. Martin ran after it waving his arms, but gave up
when he realised the Firewall must work after all. He
switched it off and breezed back to the bus stop, ready to test
it further.

As he stepped off the bus in town, he sensed that
something was wrong. The street was busy: traffic was
backed up, roadworks were under way, but he could barely
hear a thing. If he closed his eyes for a moment, he could
almost believe he was on the village High Street, far away
from the racket of the city. He retrieved the Firewall and
flicked it off. Noise engulfed him as if he had stuck his head

out the window of a moving train. He switched it back on and sank into the comfort it offered. Intrigued by the possibilities, and spurred on by new courage, he roamed the street baiting pedestrians with a provocative stare. They all blanked him. The Firewall needed a sterner test.

—Hey! he called, stepping in front of a woman, hurrying to work. She moved smartly out of the way as if he were a litter bin or small child.

—Hey! The Firewall's layer of protection really did appear to work. There was none of the furtiveness that people adopt in order to avoid being seen: Martin simply didn't exist for them.

He tried a third time, just to be certain, jumping in front of the next man he saw.

—Hoi!

The man, shorter than Martin but better built and, he quickly realised, infinitely more threatening, stopped in his tracks but didn't back off. Instead, his face remained just centimetres from Martin's own.

—Hoi! Martin shouted again.

The menace in the man's voice was underlined by the quiet calm with which he spoke.

—What are you playing at, pal? The words were slow, clear and sharp as a blade.

Martin searched for a retort but his throat felt suddenly dry. He reached into his back pocket to turn the Firewall up. Alert to the movement, the man grabbed Martin's wrist.

—Don't even think about it, he muttered.

—I wasn't; I— Martin trembled, realising there was no way he could tell the truth. He stood aside and watched the man swagger up the street. The man didn't look back.

*

It was in the office that the Firewall really proved its worth.

He could remain anonymous. Sean, his line manager, appeared from time to time to pick a volunteer for some job or other, but the higher Martin switched the Firewall, the less chance there was of being selected.

He could ignore the banality of the office chatter, of last night's TV and next weekend's football.

And — bliss! — he could stifle the noise of the telephone. Martin hated answering the phone. Years of complaints channelled down the receiver had bred a Pavlovian fear of ringtones. Now, when it rang, he would be aware of it only as the dimmest of background noises: something heard in another room, perhaps. For this reason alone he valued the Firewall.

All of which would have been ideal from the company's point of view, if in compensation Martin's focus on his job was intensified. But he quickly realised that if nobody was aware of him, then nobody was aware of him doing nothing.

After a day or two with the Firewall in his back pocket, growing warm through constant use, he suspected that his work colleagues were becoming frustrated. He could see the glances now and again, but their comments were easily filtered by switching the device to a higher setting, so he completed his working days secure behind the Firewall, largely unaware of the growing resentment in the office. It culminated in the shadow cast on his desk one afternoon by Sean's bulk. Martin hadn't noticed his approach.

−Martin? A moment please, in my office. Sean was a large man and breathed heavily, making his every sentence sound pained and impatient.

Martin followed, trudging through the wake of his boss's huge form.

−Close the door behind you.

Martin did so, and took, as indicated, a seat across the desk from Sean. His boss was red-faced and with a thick head of dark hair, the fringes of which seemed lacquered to his scalp giving him the eternal impression of having just run up three flights of stairs. Martin felt suddenly exposed.

−What are you, some kind of ostrich?

Martin was caught off-guard. −Pardon?

−An ostrich. Burying its head in the sand. Because that's what it seems like.

Martin stammered, casting about for words from which to create a defence.

−It's been communicated to me that you don't answer your phone any more. You don't respond to the fax machine. You barely acknowledge − and I've seen this myself − your colleagues' existence. Sean picked a speck of dirt from underneath an untidy fingernail. −I can't let it continue.

Martin began to sweat. Sean waited until Martin opened his mouth to protest, and continued:

–It's putting strain on the rest of the office. Five times
now, someone has been in here to complain about you.
We're busy enough just now without people—

Martin shifted in his seat. He hoped the movement made
him appear penitent and contrite, but he was straining to
reach the Firewall and slot it up to 5. In an instant, Sean's
voice became hazy and insubstantial, as ephemeral as speech
in a half-remembered dream. Martin nodded and shook his
head as he felt appropriate.

*

By the weekend, Martin had left the Firewall on for so long
– turning it off only when he went to sleep – that he had
already replaced the batteries, and hadn't even used the
stealth setting yet. But the expense of batteries was nothing
to the benefits of the device. He breezed through each day,
feeling nothing of the stress of the High Street, the
discomfort of the daily commute, nor the increasing tensions
of his workplace, which Sean's warning had failed to defuse.
In fact, Martin felt almost nothing at all.

There was a phone number on the Firewall's packaging
to encourage customer feedback and, so pleased was he with
the success of the device, he considered calling the company
to give a glowing report. His hand even got as far as to lift
the handset, but as he did so he felt a sensation, like a shiver
down the spine. It was a vague presentiment of discomfort,
attached to the telephone, that he couldn't quite articulate,
as if the machine was to be distrusted, but he couldn't
remember why – it seemed merely irrelevant. He unplugged
the phone and hid it in a drawer.

Meanwhile, his mobile displayed the details of calls he'd
missed. Text messages piled up from friends and family, his
sister Maggie in particular, but somehow they didn't seem
urgent any more. They were like those tiny fruit flies that
increasingly inhabited his flat, feeding on food that had
passed its sell-by date: a nuisance to be crushed when he
noticed.

*

On Saturday afternoon, the door buzzed and he was gripped
by real fear. The blood rushed to his face and his hands
tingled. All other invasions of his space he could filter or

smother, but actual visitors were rare, so he hadn't considered the front door to be vulnerable. His heart drummed a spasmodic beat as he peered through the spyhole. He recognised the sharp haircut of his sister. Maggie rang again. She might, he supposed, give up and leave after a while but the windows were open and the TV chattered away to itself in the living room.

—Marty? Marty, its me. Are you there?

His sweaty fingers struggled to clasp the Chubb lock as he fumbled the door open.

—Marty. She looked disappointed to note that he was clean-shaven, fully dressed and to all appearances normal. —I was worried. Is everything okay? You haven't returned anyone's calls or answered the phone in days.

—I'm fine. Never better, in fact. Thanks. He gripped the edge of the door.

—Let me in, then.

He moved aside, and closed the door after her. He hesitated, then turned back and pulled the chain across.

—What's wrong? Maggie stood in the kitchen, hand on a slender hip, surveying the ostensible normality that surrounded her younger brother.

—*Nothing*.

—Marty ... you've not murdered someone, have you? And locked them in the fridge? She swung open the fridge door, inspected the freezer compartment. —Well, that's something, I suppose.

—I'm fine, really. I promise you. There is nothing bothering me. Nothing at all.

Maggie filled the kettle and regarded her brother while it boiled. His vacant stare sparked into life as he realised he'd no idea how long she'd been watching him. She folded her arms in the way their mother would when she'd had enough, a growing look of exasperation on her face.

—How are things? he asked, blinking himself awake.

—Are you really interested?

Martin winced as if he'd been scratched. —What's wrong?

Maggie found two mugs and angrily heaped coffee granules into them.

—It's work. We've been downsized.

The kettle snapped off and she started to pour. —We're

being made redundant at the end of the year and production is being outsourc— oh, FUCK!

She'd dropped the kettle. The lid popped off and boiling water spilled across the worktop. Maggie jumped back, wringing her hands.

−Fuck! Sorry. She leaned over to the cold tap and held a finger beneath the stream. −I've … I wanted to speak to you but you never answer. (−Idiot, she muttered, looking down at the puddle of steaming water cascading to the floor.)

Martin's hand shot to his back pocket. He stood by the kitchen door, gazing at the waterfall. Maggie's cry continued to bounce off every hard surface.

−It's okay, he mumbled. −Everything's okay. Everything's okay.

−Martin? Maggie's gaze shifted between the spilled water, her scalded fingers and the pitiful form of her brother cowering by the door.

−Martin? He didn't respond, didn't move. She took his arm and led him, compliant, into the living room. The TV news was on. −I'll clean up, don't worry. Will you tell me what's going on?

Like a schoolboy whose secret has been uncovered, Martin pulled the Firewall from his pocket.

−What is it?

As he explained, he turned it over between his palms like an amulet.

−Christ, Marty, you're going to become a hermit. Get a grip.

−But it makes things so much easier.

−No. No it doesn't. It just puts them off, and they get more complicated. What have you got to hide from? Don't be so damn weak.

−You should try it. If you're worried about your job—

−If I'm *worried* about my job I might do something about it. If I use that I'll just drift along docile until the severance pay comes through. It's good to worry now and again. It's what makes you fight. What are you turning into?

Martin groaned and, cupping the Firewall in his sweaty hands, nudged it up to 5. He sank into the settee, barely conscious of Maggie's presence, or her exit. The door slammed a hundred metres away. He watched the shapes and colours and patterns of the news. They reminded him of something, almost like they should have meaning, but he couldn't quite remember what.

*

The three work colleagues sat around the circular table in the staff room, picking at their lunches. Two of them sat on one side — Dennis and Kathy, she as loud as he was quiet — turning the pages of the newspaper they were reading. She was married, he was divorced, and their office romance had briefly been the talk of the workplace. While they still, for obvious reasons, carried on with an air of the illicit, to their colleagues the liaison was stale news, almost distasteful. However, like all those freshly in love, believing there to be an aura of the untouchable about their union, they were surprised when Martin had slunk into the chair across from them. But as he continued to behave in the distracted, absent fashion of his which had replaced their affair as the topic of workplace gossip, they ignored his presence and concentrated on the newspaper.

Another war was brewing. The government was recycling the lies and excuses used to start the last one, hoping no-one would notice. Kathy shook her head in outrage.

—I can't believe it. Her voice was loud in the small kitchen. Martin looked up in alarm. —Do they think nobody will notice?

—Notice what? asked Martin.

—This. She pushed the newspaper towards him. He gazed at it blankly. It was full of large headlines and threatening language he couldn't bring himself to interrogate.

—Best not to worry about it, he said, the words coming out strangled and uneven. —I'm sure it'll all get sorted out.

Aware of, but bewildered by, the incredulous stare of the other two, Martin had a momentary sense of the distance grow between the two sides of the table, as if the plastic separating them had stretched to infinity. Maggie's words came to mind. He reached into the back pocket and hesitated, finger touching the *on/off* switch but not quite daring to press. Dennis, he saw, was watching him with something approaching concern. Quickly, Martin pressed the button and rejoined the world of his colleagues.

—Are you coming to the pub tonight? Dennis asked.

Martin hadn't been aware there was a works' night out but he nodded hurriedly.

—Yes. Yes, of course.

He couldn't catch the barman's eye, nor was there room at the packed bar to reach into his pocket and feel if the Firewall was on. Sometimes, he reflected, you were invisible whether you liked it or not. He glanced across to where his workmates sat huddled on stools around a small table. His own stool had been claimed while he was waiting at the bar.

The party moved on to a nightclub. The alcohol settled its own form of security on his brain but it wasn't the same: he knew the feeling of invincibility was all in his head. The Firewall was for real.

It happened in a corner of the nightclub. Kathy's husband had turned up with some friends, and spied his wife with Dennis. Martin saw him, short but wiry and somehow familiar, advance on Dennis. Martin's hand went to his back pocket. The man saw the movement. A sudden shock of recognition.

—I know your face, pal. Okay, I'll take the both of you, then.

Martin slid the Firewall to *stealth*. For a moment, he thought it hadn't worked: the man still advanced. But, he realised as he sank into the electronic device's synthetic balm, the man was advancing on Dennis, not him. He didn't even see the knife, just a functional, efficient move of the wrist, like you'd expect in a kitchen. The crowd melted away and one of their party screamed.

Martin recoiled from the grasping hands of the body at his feet. They were nothing to do with him. The mouth moved, opening and closing emptily, but Martin heard nothing. The only sensation he felt, stirring somewhere in the dimness of his mind, was the itch of something he might once have called guilt. He looked at the Firewall but already it was up as high as it could go, and nothing would shift the feeling.

Kate Hendry

THE SLASHING OF WEE FRASER

It's been nearly five years since I was last here. I swore I was over it – it's for young ones, this way of life. I'd like to say I'm doing time for someone else, but I've got to hold my hands up to it. This time really is the last though. I know they all say that and you've no reason to believe me – every sentence is the last, isn't it? But it is different – the fight changed everything. Well, not so much the fight itself, it was no surprise, but how well I knew the script.

You'd think you wouldn't get used to it. A lot's changed at Barlinnie after all – slopping out for a start. Though that just gives the screws another reason to keep you banged up all day. There's TVs now too, in every peter, which also keeps us quiet. And of course there's much more smack. That suits the screws too. Junkies, even those who just indulge during jail time, don't make violent cons.

To start with you notice all the differences. You go around telling folk how it was in the old days. They're not interested, the new boys, why would they be? The ones just out of the Y.O.s want to know if you're holding anything. The others, the ones who've been in and out enough to have heard it all, just want to know if you're any good with a pool cue.

There's no one to tell about how much it's changed so you stop noticing. Then you get to be a pass man. You know the system, you keep your head down, you're no longer young and jumping off the walls. You don't take any shit. So you get a job on the pass. A Hall, second flat, cleaning. You get your door open most of the day and boys at it every other minute wanting something. Toothpaste, shaving gel, J Cloths. It's unreal, the number of J Cloths you hand out.

So you're in your routine and every day's the same, except weekends when you're banged up most of the day. And it feels like you've been here forever and you can't remember what it was like before the TVs came, when you called the screws sir, when you spent all day, every day locked in your peter, listening to the radio, or your co-pilot shitting in a bucket.

Months go past like this. You don't count when your

sentence is years not months. No one wears a watch here, they keep time for you. You move through the halls. A Hall when you arrive. B Hall for a while. E Hall so you can't settle, then D Hall for good behaviour. There your section's only two flats high, not the four storeys of the other halls. The walls are painted lilac. The panels along the landings, that stop you falling to your death, are made of perspex, not metal mesh. The kind of things that really matter. The cleaning's the same though and the other cons still want your J Cloths.

All time inside's like this. When you're young you develop preferences – the dorms of Low Moss, the drugs at Kilmarnock, the food at Glenochil. But then you realise it's all the same. You move from hall to hall, from jail to jail if you're doing long enough. It breaks the time up – for a while things seem different – but your days pass just the same in every jail. Eating, sleeping, maybe some courses to up your chance of parole, and work. If you're in a shed – joinery, textiles, concrete – mostly work is an extended tea break and playing cards. Endless games of Bella, it's the only game you play. If you're on the pass it's mostly chatting. Nine quid a week, you don't put yourself out for that.

My main job in D Hall was cleaning the showers. I normally did it mid-morning when everyone's out at work. But this one day I was late, and it made all the difference. The screws had me talking to the visiting committee. They like to have them talk to the intelligentsia, as they call the likes of me. So when I got up there with my mop and pail it was just after lunch and there were boys milling about. Sitting in each others' cells, smoking and playing Bella. Queuing for the phone, chatting up the screws.

I saw the two boys going into the peter opposite the showers. Mick, one of them's called. Not much more than a Y.O. The other wasn't long in and I didn't know his name. He was about the same age. Colin came out almost immediately. He looked at me. He's older, like me, in his thirties, not stupid. Probably can't take any more of the pish the younguns talk, I thought. Colin's been dubbed up with a kid, wee Fraser. Can't keep his mouth shut. He's been doing Colin's head in, but he's out soon so he puts up with it. Colin tried to warn him, told him to settle down, but it didn't stop him from going on at folk. Looking for a fight, that's how he came across, though probably he was just trying to make friends.

So when these two went in I thought, briefly, that maybe he'd found some playmates. But the look on Colin's face told me wee Fraser had probably just taken it too far with the wrong people. I filled my pail and got on with the job. No point getting involved. I did feel a bit sorry for the wee boy though, so I thought I'd better keep an eye out, check his new mates didn't go too far. I watched through the mirrors at the back of the shower block. They fill up the whole wall.

It happened fast; these things usually do. Mick pulled out a chib – a home-made job, a razor blade melted into the end of a plastic toothbrush. Can be lethal. His sidekick pinned Fraser to the back wall. I could see his face flinching from side to side, like a baby refusing to eat his porridge. His eyes and mouth tight shut. Mick slashed his face and backed away almost in the same moment, to keep clear of the spray of blood. The sidekick let Fraser drop. Blood spurted through Fraser's fingers as he tried to hold his cheek together. I could hear him trying to hold in the scream. A high-pitched gurgle as if he was gagged.

As soon as his pals were away I hit the alarm button and went across to him. He couldn't speak. I think he was afraid to open his mouth in case his face fell apart. The cut went almost to the edge of his lips. I had a wad of J Cloths with me and I held them against his face until the screws ran in.

I've seen it dozens of times before. Less as a con admittedly, but it amounts to the same thing whoever's involved. And, as I said, wee Fraser had it coming. Maybe he'd settle down after this. That's what I was thinking as I went back to my cell for the inevitable lock-up after a fight.

I lay on my bed and closed my eyes. I went over it again, watching it happen in the mirror. A mirror wet from the showers, so the edges of the figures were blurred. There had been no sounds. Or at least they'd been drowned out by the shouting, laughing cons all around. It was as if it had been rehearsed, it all went so smoothly. They played their parts perfectly, even wee Fraser, scared as his mouth filled with blood, took the blade as best as his reflexes would let him and sank to the floor to wait for help.

It was like seeing a rerun of a cheap ITV crime drama,

played out once more just for my benefit. I was the only audience, though I don't expect they cared about witnesses. You don't grass, if you've got any self-respect. It was entirely predictable, the chain of events – like I was a second or two ahead of it – unsurprised by the blade, the cut, the blood. As if I knew how wee Fraser was going to react, as if I was telling him what to do next – hold your arms up, back away, close your eyes, twist your head away, swallow your scream, crumple. He did everything I told him to.

It gave me a shock, that. Not the violence or the blood – you get immune to that during your very first sentence. It was the way I knew it all so well. The certainty of it. Like realising there's no surprises left, life has nothing unexpected to offer you. I had been here too many times.

In the days after the fight, when I wasn't being interrogated by the screws, I tested myself out. How often could I guess what was going to happen. The boy on the phone to his missus, monosyllables, then silence, then shouting. She hangs the phone up at her end, he bashes the phone against the wall. Cons shout at him – it's the only phone. The boy droning on about the women he's pulled. Who'll be the first to have had enough? Who'll walk away, who'll tell him he's a prick? Which cocky newcomer will wind up the screws? Which ones have brought drugs in? I guessed what ten were in for and got them all right.

I got moved off the pass a couple of days after the fight. For my own safety, the screws said, but they were hoping it'd wind me up and I'd grass. I had a couple of weeks on concrete – my punishment. Making the shafts that go underneath manhole covers. I've done it before. It's shite but you get on with it. Don't let them know they've got to you. Bide your time and it changes soon enough.

A few weeks after that they'd forgotten and I got a job on the garden party. In the summer it's the best job in the jail as you're outdoors all day. I thought maybe working with plants, I'd find something to surprise me. The wonder of nature. But jail nature is sprayed with pesticides and fertilisers till it has to conform. I'd been on vegetable duty for a while, then extra bodies were needed for watering the hanging baskets, now the flowers were out. I suppose I just hadn't noticed them, walking to work. And I didn't realise how many there were till I had to water them. Each hall had a dozen of them, in a zigzag pattern above the door and a further four on each side of the door. Even the digger has a huge basket of trailing nasturtiums and begonias on either side of its entrance. The last living thing you see before you're banged up on your own for days or weeks on end. As the summer went on the flowers bloomed bigger and brighter. The jail was covered in them.

Probably it was just a way of creating work for us over the summer, but it looked as if they were trying to cover up the jail. The funny thing was, the more flowers there were the more I could see the jail. The halls weren't just the various dormitories I'd kipped in. They were monster stone sheds. Twenty-six octagonal chimneys, like a rank of watch-towers growing out of slate roofs. Above the hanging baskets each hall had a single arched window, like in a church, scaling the height of the building. The windows were segmented into narrow strips of old glass; thick, opaque.

Back in the hall at night I started to examine the windows. I hadn't thought much about them before. That's because most of them don't open. The few that do only open an inch – enough to tempt and frustrate you. In most halls the glass is so scratched you can't see out. We're the lucky ones. D Hall was refurbished last year, so we can see out of our windows. Three strips of glass, two inches by ten. From one side you can see C Hall and from the other the screws' carpark. You watch them leaving, going home at the end of the day to their families. You wish you could slash their tyres. Mostly, though, the windows in the jail are there so the authorities can cut back on light bulbs. Why would a con want to see out? Better he doesn't know what he's missing. The new boys in D Hall complain about being able to see out. They fix newspaper over their windows and old bits of cloth. They'd rather live in the dark.

Windows aren't windows in the jail. And roads aren't roads either. They look like them to start with. The main one, through the jail, has even got pavements. A lorry goes up and down delivering food to the halls. And there's a red Massey Ferguson tractor with a green trailer that collects the rubbish. A pickup brings wood to the joinery sheds and sleek silver Vauxhalls chauffeur the management. There's pedestrians too, like on any normal street; social workers, psychologists, teachers, all looking like ordinary people. Some smile at you, some look down. The tarmac's patched in places, one section dug up and coned off. Steam pours out of a manhole. Streetlights, a black feral cat — just like an ordinary street.

Except there's no houses; just these vast Victorian mills, factories with coils of barbed wire on their roofs and drainpipes encased in metal sheaves, so no one can climb up or down. The front doors have no knockers, bells or letter boxes. All is quiet on jail street, except at set times, four times a day, when the blue doors open and the screws, peaked hats sitting low on their foreheads, come out of their bunkers and position themselves in a long line, a few feet apart, down the length of the road. Then the prisoners pour out, in their red jumpers, ready to be herded to work or to their hall for feeding time.

The jail doesn't sound like the real world either. The seagulls screech, though we're miles from the sea. Their cries overlap the coos of the pigeons who roost on window ledges and send ropes of white shit down the walls. There's always keys rattling somewhere — against other keys, against chains, in locks. Gates are dragged open, metal doors bounce against their frames before locking shut. Walkie-talkies crackle, the generator hums. Someone whistles, screws shout in the halls or outside; a name, a command. Cons in the digger yell to keep each other company.

My company, for months, had been a quiet nervy boy. He watched TV and jiggled his feet and occasionally asked for tobacco when he'd smoked all his. Then he left suddenly. I came back from work to find a new boy unpacking. Bigger, slower, older. Jail tattoos on his hands and arms, meaningless blue lines and shapes.

'Alright,' he said when I came in, 'name's Davy.'

I introduced myself and offered to shake his hand. He took it but looked surprised.

'Not your first time, is it?' he asked suspiciously.

'This is my twelfth sentence,' I replied. He relaxed a bit.

'I'm catching up on you,' he grinned, 'this is my eleventh. Only a six moon though. Breach of parole and housebreaking. Got a concurrent. Good brief.' He rolled a cigarette and climbed up on his bunk.

'What time's rec here?' he called down.

I filled him in on the regime. How many times have I

had this conversation, I wondered. I turned the TV on to cut it short and Davy settled into an abusive address to the characters on *Neighbours*.

It was bright outside. The dirty glass stops any ray of sunshine coming through but a misty glow of light still filled the cell. I tried to push my hand out of the open side panel.

'You don't wanna do that,' called down Davy from his bunk. 'A pigeon might crap on you.'

I withdrew my arm.

'I don't want to be here any more,' I said.

'You and me both, mate,' replied Davy, staring at the TV.

I turned the sound down, it was suddenly important to explain.

'You don't understand. I don't want to be *here* any more.'

'Oh, you mean you're looking for a transfer. I'm hoping to get to Glenochil. Supposed to be good up there.' He looked a bit annoyed to be missing the end of his pro- gramme, but you don't complain when you're second in.

'It's not that, it just doesn't make sense any more.'

'Never did mate, never did. Weekend dubup's long here.' He tried to reassure me as if I was going mad from claustrophobia.

'I heard we could all be moving. They're painting this hall, that'll cheer you up. Tell you what, we could smash the TV before we go then they'll give us a new one. The remote's fucked on this one. Turn the sound up.'

I did as he wanted and went back to the window. If I leant against the wall I could just see out of the open panel. A strip of yellow stone from the opposite hall. I counted six separate stones. A seagull swooped across. The yellow greyed as a cloud covered the sun briefly then came through again. A crumpled wrapper zigzagged to the ground. A plastic bottle fell next with a flash of Irn-Bru orange. Then a bunch of cards, red and black flickering. Someone not happy with their hand. An alarm clock began to ring. No one brings a clock into the jail, except old men and fraudsters. It went on ringing. I couldn't tell where it was coming from. Someone wanted to wake up, gone five o'clock in the afternoon. Someone was sleeping deeply. It wasn't me.

Vicki Husband

MASLOW

Coming down from Crosshead that day I knew there'd been an accident. When I saw the circle of people, heads bent inward, I knew it was Maslow. Right away I knew. It was his patch; the traffic island opposite the bus shelters, on Parkside. The ambulance had already been called. I leaned out the window to see if I could help but I was working, what could I do? They said it was a truck, no a car, a truck. Didnae sound good. Jim was waiting to jump on shift so he'd seen it near enough. Said they took Maslow to the Royal but he didnae know the ward. I phoned later that night to find out.

Maslow's the guy who directs the buses. You'll have seen him. Standing on that island like the traffic polis waving the buses past, gieing the drivers jip for no reason, patrolling his pitch, cursing like a daemon. But mostly he's harmless: he winks a lot, Maslow, that's how you know. There's a guy that directs the buses in every city. There was one in Manchester who was a right bampot. Cannae mind his name. He could get quite aggressive if he took you the wrong way. No like Maslow, aw bark nae teeth.

I swithered whether to go to the hospital aw that day and aw the next. I hate hospitals but I kept thinking what if he died without anyone visiting him. I kept thinking a truck, no a car. And I imagined his body folded, on the road, like I'd seen it which I hadn't. Well not his body but his coat I kept seeing, in a heap, the one he always wears, even on the hot days, a gabardine he calls it. Sometimes he put a fluorescent waistcoat over the top, Chief gave him a corporation one as a kind of a joke, the health and safety thing; him always back and forth across the road, high stepping that left leg with the drop foot. It was an auld yin. When he wore it he made a big point of telling you, like you could miss it.

I asked the lads if any of them were going to see Maslow. Maist of them said no or made an excuse then said no and John said what the fuck you want to visit him for? The McVey Bus boys said they'd whip round for a card. They never did but it gave me the idea. I bought one and signed the names myself, Maslow would never tell the difference. I chose some of the names he'd know: Jim and Reager and Neilsie. Then added a few more that I made up: Rab and Ian and Billy; there's always a Billy.

My shift that day seemed long and the punters did ma heid in. Every one of them was trying to con us out of a few pence and naebdy had bothered to renew their passes. That always annoys me, they know when it's due up so what's their problem? I'd heard all the excuses. I was always tough on the pass dodgers. Unless they looked like they might batter us then I'd let it go. I was stuck twice at Parkside in a jam, once on the way up, once on the way down. Seemed strange Maslow no being there. The place was chaos, he'd have loved that. Walking upside the drivers' windaes letting them aw know what was going on. Directing them past each other in turn, like we didnae dae that aw day every day without his help. But we aw let him direct us, saluted him on the way past. A mark of respect like for the auld yin; the crazy fella.

I'd spoke to Maslow only a few weeks before he got knocked down. I remember that I'd finished my shift and handed over to Neilsie at the Cross. It was muggy that day, really muggy and I fancied a pint. I saw Maslow on the island so I waved. He returned it with his salute. That you off shift son, he shouted over and glanced at his watch to check my sign off time. Habit probably; never leaves you. I walked over to him, want to come for a pint Maslow? I said. Bold as you like, it's no really like me to be social but it was a muggy day and I felt sorry for him, daft old bugger and I reckoned he'd have some rare stories that would go down well with the pint. No son, he said, I'm on a late shift the night, and he walked off to give the new Polish driver a rollicking for something or other. That's when I decided he was crazy. It's one thing to keep going past retirement, doing a bit of voluntary, pretending to be one of the lads for the company and that but inventing late shifts for yourself? That's beyond me.

The wife was out at the karaoke again on the Saturday so I decided, spur of the moment, just to go up to the Royal. Like I said though, I really hate hospitals. The Royal is enough to put you off ever being ill, it's a dirty auld pile like something out a Gothic horror film except never deserted.

Always full of shapes under blankets, in wheelchairs, on trolleys. Everyone is tornfaced except the nurses and doctors. I've never understood that, why they always look so cheery. Like they're enjoying the suffering. It makes me nervous.

I went to the admissions ward first but they told me that he'd moved to 23. Wouldnae tell me what was wrong with him because I wasn't family. I thought then that I might not get to see him unless I was family. I reckoned that he didn't have anybody. A man like that, always bloody working or else kipping on the benches asides Cross Park. I thought it would have been a wasted journey otherwise so I decided to say I was a cousin; no harm in being a cousin.

I goes up to ward 23, aw those stone steps and the smell and the doctors laughing and smiling with each other and I says who I was here to see and I says I'm his cousin. So this ginger-haired nurse walks me up the ward and I thought I could see him in a bed at the end, all alone, hunched over a paper. Didn't have my glasses on right enough. But she turns at the top of the ward and takes me into a four-bedded room. And there's Maslow sitting on a chair, stookie on his leg, looking like a different man. He's clean-shaven and smiling and there's visitors. Maslow winks at the nurse a couple of times and she says, your cousin to see you Mr. Maslow, old fashioned like, then she leaves. Maslow's looking at me blankly and the visitors have turned round to see. Cousin? I can hear him say, I've no got a cousin that's walking this earth. The visitors are staring at me now: a youngish woman with a bairn on her knee and a man near enough my age.

There was no sign of recognition on Maslow's face so I decides to bolt. Wrong bed, I say a couple of times, sorry I say a couple of times and back out the room with the visitors still swivelling their heads and staring. Wrong bloke, I half shout at the ginger nurse as I pass her on my way out. I take the stone steps two at a time and wait for the sixty-six outside. Reager comes belting around the corner so fast that he almost doesnae see me. It was all down to an idjit blocking a lane back at Newton Road, he tells me. I stand by the driver's cab but I don't know Reager very well and he doesn't know me so we soon run out of conversation. He asks who I've been to see in the Royal. An old aunt, I say, she's no well. And then he asks about Maslow, smiling as he says, did yi hear onything? No, I say, no. He'll be back directing the buses in no time, Reager says. I realise then that I still have the card in my pocket and I crush it in my sweaty hand. Maybe not, I say, it was a truck, no a car, a truck.

Fiona Jack

THE RINGS

Death uncorks time,
Releases selves
From their place
On the line of history.
You are no more old woman
Than playful child.

A young woman,
The one my father
Speaks of most,
Slips thin as a wafer
Between my thoughts.
A stranger,
She comes from the years
Before mine.

I find her
In a cotton dress
On a hill of sand,
Or posing with my father
Tilted towards him.
She sits laughing on a bridge
Swinging her legs
Above the stream.
Her fingers flicker a greeting.

Young woman,
I have your ring.
A Shetland shawl passes through
A wedding ring,
But only the finest web
Could slip through
This gold circle.

Different from the other,
A wider band
For thickened joints.
The one I twisted gently
On a hand
Turned to stone.

Andy Jackson

AIR BAND RADIO

Each Friday, softened by wages,
he came home early
and lay dissolving his worker's grime,
the water rising and falling with his breath,
lapping in sympathy with the buzz
of his radio—
Not music but chatter
from the control tower,
the cocky few flying in for the weekend.
He knew their business—
diverted souls bound for Blackpool
or weathered out of Ringway,
in shells small enough to drop steeply
onto the green moss pasture
across the canal.

His sons passed out in rigid blue,
rank upon rank upon rank,
starting a life he might have wanted as his own.
He never saw himself in them
or them in him.

Crisply clothed in clean dusk air,
he watched alone from the turf below the tower,
stood at the wrong end of his binoculars,
his radio hissing gently on the car bonnet.
Noisy, tiny aircraft stooged above,
little wings, diamonds in the sky,
gleaming with every dip of their nose.
The mystery of their glass and silver skins
turned to china-cloth and plywood,
such a disappointment when you got close.

Mary Johnston

KISTED

Fit wye wis he kisted bare heided
an rowed in a fite satin shrood?

he only iver fupt aff his bonnet
ti flapt ower a saaser o tay

grandad aye wore scuddlin claes
ald dungars an tackety beets:

wis his waadin an funeral
navy blue shuit

lookt ower bi grunny for mochs
nae gweed eneuch for aat day?

Fit wye wis he kisted bare heided
an rowed in a fite satin shrood?

Helen Lamb

MID-SUMMER NIGHT RIFF

When darkness hid
Below the bed
Dad sat late at the piano
Ignoring drowsy neighbours
Restless child above
The silken hours winding
Into fragile midnight

Everything he knew
Was in the present riff
Heavy on the bass
Fast and sweet on the roll
His left foot pounding through it all
Until the deep, blue thud
Became the heartbeat of the house

Louise Laurie

GINGERBREAD MEN

We'd decided on a slice
of seaside life
—sedate, quite ordinary
tucked away
by geography
going about its business
apologetically.

We did the usual things
in between the rain—
walked along the prom
gorged on ice cream
and cursed the gulls
as plump as cats.

Suddenly – we saw it—
a Moby Dick look-a-like.
Black as seaweed
and a periscope to match.
We held our breath.
It held our eyes.

It must have surfaced
behind our backs
(how could we have missed it?)
and now the shiny, slimy thing
was slinking past yachts
and pleasure craft.

Its peelie-wally crew
at ease, all at sea
on its giant, humped spine
like a perfect row
of dough gingerbread men.

Submerged in thought
we shivered
in the summer heat.

Peter Maclaren

RETURN TO SUTHERLAND

Was it twelve years ago,
that midnight walk through the pines,
the blazing fish boxes on the white shore
throwing sparks into a black sky
(Vestey's beach, of course – who else?
but not his sky)
while the Atlantic slid on the shingle
ten yards from the flames.

Now the village halls are built of stone,
the dog-leg roads are twisted straight,
their turf edges fade into a paler green.
Once a month, just for a look,
a town optician drives here,
to hold a surgery.

Mere scratches on a landscape, these.
No trains within fifty miles,
only the ebb and flow of water.
The *Diadem*, rounding the point to Clash,
oily wheelhouse riding the spray
as the land opens, offering harbour.
In the toilets at the dance
– a Friday for fear of the Lord –
half bottles still change hands,
and the way to the ferry
lies sprinkled with the first snow of winter,
fieldfares and redwings
swooping low over the lochan,
the winking beercan in the ditch,
bright under Suilven's shadow.

Near Sheigra,
the last house on the mainland
is offered for sale
– in the Post Office window
beside a notice for silk flowers.

Light drains from a thin sky,
a heap of ash blows on a northern beach
so much time spun
so many years unwound.

Ciara MacLaverty

PAST LOVE IN THE MUSEUM OF TRANSPORT

Where's Daddy?
I say, holding your son in my arms,
inhaling the baby scent of his head.
You're up on the steam engine
with your other son
pointing, waving down at us.

You still look good
and I can hold your gaze
without fear of loss
or fear of holding on.

Drinking tea in the café
I ask about your wife
and say how patient
and good-natured your kids are.
You clean the baby's face
and use the wet wipe to sweep
the mess from the formica table.

I wonder how we ever fought,
how anyone ever fights,
and I am soothed
and oddly grateful
that it's come to this

like tracing my
fingertips over a smooth scar
healed to the point where—
almost imperceptibly—
it reflects
more light.

Andy Manders

FALLERS

The body when he found it wasn't unlike the ones he'd seen pictures of sticking out of the ice when the glaciers retreated. He wouldn't have found it at all but for a break in the clouds that had draped themselves about the hills since morning, casting sudden thick shafts of sunlight along the Bad Dearg perimeter. Drawn by the play of light on the panels he'd pulled the Landy onto the verge and, once he'd raked in his pack for the camera, set off down towards the fence like a tourist. The minute he caught sight of it hanging there amidst the tatters of its clothing, ribboned like Buddhist prayer flags, he knew that, whatever else, it'd force him to think. And this barren bloody bog wasn't ever gonna be the place for that.

Most of the fallers, fried remains scraped from the glass within half an hour of their landing, hardly merited a second thought; never even got the chance to weather, but this one, instead of triggering the alarm, had somehow contrived to get itself snagged on the wire. It looked like it'd been there a while.

At the same time the heat off the glass, combined with the night-time cold, seemed to have achieved much the same preserving effect as Alpine freezing. It must have dried the skin before any wee beasties could get properly acquainted, which meant the flesh below had had time to cook, then slowly to begin to waste – the fences having seen off the local carrion-eating wildlife. Even the craws, God knows why, must have left it pretty much alone. So it looked – apart from the scarring you'd expect, a vertebra or two jarringly out of place, and the context (and the time it'd been there of course) – like there wasn't that much wrong with it really.

On the other hand it was the first in a long time and it gave him quite a turn. The first female he could remember too, though he'd heard there'd been others, one on the Inverness side at the turn of the year. He'd just been lucky. It made it worse somehow, a woman, however you rationalised it. Quite apart from that, and the weathering and the time it'd been there, caught magically in mid-air above the banks of glass, was the positioning of its limbs.

She'd obviously struggled to free herself, and had as a result ended up bizarrely enveloped in the twists. Though you couldn't see it now, he knew she'd be every bit as sliced and torn from the razor-wire as the clothes she'd been wearing. Her arms and legs were tucked together and curled up like she might have been sleeping. If you really pushed it, from the spread fingers of the hand nearer her face, you could imagine her stretching to smooth the hair back from her face, or sucking her thumb mibbe.

He'd never seen one on the wire before, never heard of it even. It wasn't meant to happen; if anyone had thought about it at all, it'd have been considered impossible. He wasn't sure if they planned for that. She had. She'd done well, a real acrobat, he'd no idea how she'd got that far – another few metres and she'd have made it. At some point she must have wondered that too: if she really would. The moment when hope realises itself. Inching her way along the pylon in the dark, she must have known she was almost there. And then what? From what he could see she hadn't had much with her, which meant she'd probably have been disappointed however far she got. He smiled to himself: not prayer flags so much as the rags he remembered as a boy, tied to the fairy tree above the village; like something from the trenches it was.

Plus, getting her down wouldni be a picnic. He heard himself cursing noisily and stopped. He moved closer. Aye she was dead alright. Na, what it was was the weight had bent the wire where normally he'd go in. It'd need a good half section cut before lifting her could even be considered. Why bother? All he really needed to do was report it. He could drive back down or he could radio for back-up – the copter'd be here in ten minutes – one or the ither. Yet, predictable as ever, even before he'd set off across the bog to call from the Landy, he could see himself trudging back with his gear.

Twice he'd to go back for extra cutting rods. It'd taken him near an hour and he had no real idea why he was doing it. He'd been there before, right enough. It'd take at least as long fixing back the wire, if he was to do it properly. Which he might. The suit made him sweat and he kept needing to take breaks to take in more fluid. Inside the gloves his fingers ached.

He was glad of the breaks: working in such proximity to the body he found himself overwhelmed after no more than a few minutes. It wasn't easy to say what it was; it certainly wasn't nausea, or fear, or anything like that, or to do with her at all really. Concentrating on the cutting he was fine, till gradually there grew in him each time a sense of increasing and persistent dislocation. At first it was no more than an image of the hill-line to the west and he'd be aware of a nagging need in a moment to glance up towards it, then he'd begin to experience a sense of rapid crashing movement, of the land hurtling powerfully around him and a gathering terror that only pulling himself up from the wire and looking around him could dispel.

It was something to do with being alone. He wondered if he was afraid of dying — it seemed to be about that — and was surprised to discover he'd never asked himself this before. There'd been the time he'd hit the deer where the Foss Road cut across one of their routes right enough, but that was different. You'd see them there, at the dip by the lochan, crossing or feeding, and one night he hit one. He thought he remembered it jumping, louping from the wood but he wasn't sure; he did remember thinking it must have frozen in the lights, and that he'd done the same. It'd gone on forever like that, slipping time. You could do anything to it — dismantle it, paint it, write theses about it, pull it apart — but you couldn't change it for a second, and at some point you'd just have to lift your finger and let it go, back. Meanwhile, waiting in the wings, physics was already sorting out the particulars.

But the thing he remembered the most was the way the radio went. It was the dip in the hills, he'd noticed it before, all the way up the reception was crap. But it didn't sound like that, it sounded like the moment before there had been glorious singing and from now on, silence.

He really should be home.

It was different when they landed on the glass. Cheerier. Automatic the minute the voltage surge lit the position of the faller on the screen. They were never any bother to find. Getting them off the panels was easy. Unless it was the Drumossie section, you could figure on something under an hour there and back. And Drumossie was scheduled for upgrade soon; they'd probably end up tarring it. The whole thing was built on teamwork, each man pulling his weight, disciplined and focused, not letting the others down. You couldni take the piss oot of that. You wouldni.

Help would have been good now, to hold the wire while he cut, hand him the water, make a joke of it as best they could, mibbe even talk. The road back down was accepted as the only place you could talk. Even then it was always as much about the road and the weather as it was the faller. There were strict rules. Basically, you had to either keep your mouth shut, or a reasonable distance: you could be interested to the point of enthrallment, but you never forgot it was a game. Of two halves probably. Still a relief, still therapeutic, still guid though, above the rattle of the engine, to compare what they'd seen, swap theories about emerging patterns and statistics. And always, no matter who he was with or what had come before, there was a moment of quiet when he presumed they each thought about it. He'd noticed too that, no matter who he was with, it was always he who broke the silence.

When she fell he had to think to know if she'd made a sound at all, it was that quiet. As well as softening the landing, the heather clumps pushed aside to welcome her body before springing back, almost concealing her, so that for a second he wondered where she'd gone.

He found a stone and eased himself down. She certainly blended in. For a moment he wondered about leaving her. Presumably she'd rot eventually, become one with the earth – they were into that – and no one would know. He could pretend she wasn't there till he forgot. He could start now – he was good at forgetting – he could concentrate on the hill opposite and the Sitka ranks growing up it, he could think about the rain, anticipate its falling, welcome it. He could go home. And they'd be there on the steps to welcome him, as he'd welcomed the rain, the wee one in her arms, Catriona playing, and plonking his boots on the hearth he'd look up from his luridly melancholy reading material/dram/bath/ stupor to watch her undress/feed the wee one/play the clarsach/gut the trout he'd caught – and it'd be fine. It would be as if nothing had ever happened or what had happened was separate from him. And it would go on, not happening, forever.

He was never going to leave her. Who was he kidding? He was going to have to do something. Act, even, Jesus. The Sitka were planted in a series of vast interlocking triangle shapes, interspersed with runs of larch on the slope down to the moor. The larch were just beginning to get their colour back after the winter. He couldn't see from where he was but there must be a burn in there somewhere – a line of mist hovered from a point half way up. Rocky outcrops all.

They'd be felling soon. The Sitka weren't there when he'd come up here as a kid, thirty years before the station, stalking deer with his father. Had he noticed then how the noise of his own thoughts filled the space the silence left, so that eventually they were all he heard, their rhythm, even when the rifle cracked beside him? Had he fuck. But then, on their bellies in the heather, his best stage whisper having fallen on deaf ears, Dad had had to give him a poke, jabbing a finger in the direction of the ridge where a single hind sank to the ground as the herd bounded on. His father never missed. His father had had a great-grandfather who had gone out with Charlie. Et cetera. And what, pray, would even the least of them make of this?

In truth, when he'd applied for security he couldn't stop his chest tightening as old Sandy Johnston the factor that was, in a Biblical flourish brought on by his own discomfort, introduced him to the panel as Atholl's first-born. The station managers hadn't looked particularly impressed. But they shook the hand of Atholl's first-born, whose great-great-grandfather had been out with Charlie, and offered him a start, ten bob a week. Such was the opposition of the locals, they'd have given him work whoever he was, and paid him whatever he'd have thought himself worth. And he'd have taken it gladly. As it was, as he was, it was for the bairns. And for her. He didn't ask. Then, he'd have sold his soul to the devil, and gladly, for her. And the bairns (whose great-great-great-grandfather ...). Jesus.

Steeling himself he picked her up, and, mindful of his back, lowered her gently onto the bogey. Done. If he was to take her down, there'd be time enough for a proper inspection later. It would have been interesting to see how she actually died, of course, if forensic could establish it, though he presumed it was just the combination of extreme cold, then heat, with blood loss mibbe a contributing factor.

It was interesting. You could argue the cause of death was justification for the manner of it: the station was mostly to offset increases in temperature range in the climatic zone. She'd have died anyway; he wasn't that keen.

There was a time, a couple of years in, when no one'd have given a toss if you'd just hauled them off the glass and dumped them at the side. Now everything was recorded and logged, photographed, due process observed. Except, he would point out, what was he doing out on his own – something which was supposed to be strictly forbidden in any circumstance – dragging a fucking faller half a fucking mile through sodden peat-bog on a knackirt old cart with a dodgy axle back to the Landy, eh?

Ti hell.

Across the hills the sky was darkening, purpling to the west: he'd have to get a move on. Already the air, pleasantly cooling an hour ago, felt harsh and damp. He hadn't bothered with a fleece. Leave the fucking suit on. Mibbe it was time he packed it in, mibbe it was, mibbe it was a chance to turn his keen eye to where his real talents lay – something less physical, monitoring mibbe. He'd be in his element: not much passed Atholl's first-born by.

He could remember every one. If he let them out they'd troop before him – not the ghastly procession you'd imagine – more a school-class, a fitba team or an amateur dramatic cast. And it wasn't them he remembered anyway, it was him. The first years they'd been operational there'd been dozens, kids mostly, not knowing what they'd got themselves into, or how else to get out. And that made it easier. There was something inevitable about picking the carcass off the panels that made it bearable. They were stupid, and now they're deid, aye well. Aye well, for whatever reason it got easier anyway, and then it got harder when you realised some of them were starting to be near ages with you. Mibbe thought the same thoughts, weird and distasteful though they were, mibbe could have gotten to know. Et cetera. Et cetera. And it didni stop, though it grew less. Like mibbe one day it would stop, just peter out, and there'd be no more killing. And you'd have won.

She was mibbe 50, bit less. They were usually still a bit younger than that; men. Her hair had been long, clumps of it left on the wire, almost black. 50 kilo. 60 mibbe. She'd been lean and strong, fit. A fighter. 60 kilo, eh? Through a sodding bog. Piece of piss, now, like.

By the time he got back it was dark. He cut the Landrover lights, sitting a while in the yard, waiting for the shift to end. It was lashing down. He turned on the radio and watched the rain pooling on the cinder. Mibbe a swift yin. He didn't like to keep them waiting at home.

Lynsey May

TOY MONEY

The playground dream, so carefully planned and executed, stalled and floundered only weeks after her arrival. These people were not the casually generous soldiers who had populated her childhood after the war. They may be big and blond, but their godlike benevolence was gone. Their gifts weren't fresh oranges and squashed chocolates, and natural enthusiasm wasn't the reward they demanded. Even unwanted flowers and perfume came with a price.

Writing to her friends back home she had at first tried to keep this knowledge to herself. No point shattering illusions they would probably never get the chance to test for themselves. But her disappointment was determined to spill onto the page, if only to stop them from wasting reality on a dream as she so easily could have done. She thought of herself and Aiko, who called herself Amy now, star-struck with wonder as they crouched at the side of the road watching those heavy jeeps trundle past. Holding hands and knowing for certain what their futures would hold.

She sits transcribing minutes from a meeting she wasn't allowed to speak at and pictures money. Dollars into Yen. She is briefly but blissfully unaware of the people bustling around her and Ted's eyes boring into her back. Her fingers fly over the typewriter, spelling efficiently in English even though she is thinking in Japanese.

It's hard to catch her eye when she's always looking down like that (so demure!) but I keep trying. The possible reward of a smile makes any effort worthwhile. I see her sigh gently, the air inflating her chest a little further than normal; I want to feel that breath on my face. She will never behave indecently, never cause a scene at a party, get drunk and embarrass herself and me. A whole different breed to Alison.

Susan was sent to this office as a balm to my aching soul. A secretary, receptionist and ministering angel all as one. A sugary exotic flower gracing this stuffy room. She sits at her little desk in the front, tending to the office's needs as carefully I hope she will to mine. Never mind that it sometimes becomes a bit difficult for me to concentrate when she's right there,

*in those tight skirts and almost translucent shirts, looking like
a particularly efficient schoolgirl.*

*Later, when we are better acquainted, I will persuade
her to wear one of those silky things. Those smooth but bulky
contraptions that cover them all up but look like they could
be pulled clean off with one tug in the right place. Only in the
bedroom though, nobody else would need to see, an Oriental
outfit only for my pleasure.*

*I could spend hours looking at her, drinking in the details,
swallowing her down whole. She is like a tasty nibble, a dose
of tonic. My days were infinitely longer before she arrived,
treacly and thick. I felt like nothing would ever change.
Ambition seems pointless when no one is watching. Once
Alison encouraged and inspired me, when we were still young,
before her true colours were revealed. Now I am energised
all over again.*

Sumie fosters an ever-growing distrust of Americans. She
knows they think she is stupid. Stupid by their standards
anyway. Her voice is too girly, her accent too pronounced.
At first she considered trying to wipe it out, maybe taking
classes to make her voice as lumpy and graceless as theirs,
but she had quickly decided it was pointless. No matter how
she sounded she would always look the same. She was
fortunate to have this job really and lucky for her English-
speaking father, his fluency being responsible for her own.
(M ... m ... mia nam iss Soosan) Without his tutelage she
would have been in the same shitty position as so many of
the Japanese ex-pats whose ad-hoc community she had
willingly been sucked into. Teachers as couriers, doctors
working in noodle shacks. Their garbled pidgin English
reducing them to imbeciles in American eyes. They were the
only people who called her by her real name, the only ones
she felt able to reveal it to.

*I interrupt my work to watch her stand up and smooth that
little skirt down. Brian just hinted loudly that it must be
about time for a coffee break. That is one of Susan's duties
and one that is a pleasure to watch. She doesn't normally
make one for herself, maybe it's too bitter. They drink tea
don't they? Or is that in China? Hmm, but they're pretty
much the same aren't they?*

She's all alone over here, her sponsor abandoned her or died or something. I questioned Marilyn about her a while ago. I would have asked Susan herself but I didn't want to embarrass the angel. She was a bit funny about telling me actually. Quite sweet really, but unnecessary. Obviously I would never do anything to hurt our sweet little Susan.

Whatever she is thinking makes her lips pout delightfully and I can't help imagining them doing something else. Thinking about it makes a rush of heat fly all the way up to my face but I smile and say thank you as she places the cup on my desk. I always make an effort to show I appreciate her, not like the rest of these shmucks.

Sumie is still annoyed when she sits back down. The work she is doing may be boring and unimportant but it was frustrating to be yanked asunder. Forced to satisfy the whims of lazy people. Every time she was called away her flow was broken, time was lost that could have been used more profitably. And on days when the interruptions were most frequent and she couldn't squeeze everything into the required number of hours Mr Brownlee would chastise her mildly. With a smile and often a pat on the hand, as if she 'couldn't help it, poor soul.' The older men in this place tended to treat her as though they were a tribe of incestuous uncles who would love her to wriggle onto their laps. The younger ones thought she was desperate to fuck and then ensnare them, as if she'd want an American husband now she knew what they were like.

Her movements are deft and precise. Repetition has made her so accurate she can move with machine-like speed on occasion. Becoming one with the typewriter, coaxing it to spew out other people's words faster than she can articulate her own.

(w-i-n-d u-p doll)

She feels like her thoughts and emotions have become superfluous, unnecessary in this busy environment.

Look at her go, does she move as capably in the kitchen? Cleaning? Stretching up to those hard to reach places, her top riding up exposing a thin ellipse of soft flesh. In the bedroom? God, she's gorgeous. And the best thing is she doesn't act like

she knows it. Quiet, but not stuck up like most of those bitches.
You can tell she isn't scheming ways to put you down, hurt
you.

The unhappily matron-like Marilyn from the office upstairs
has come to distract Sumie again. The simpering, traitorous
fool. Sumie used to think she was harmless, but now she
hates her. Trapped in a cubicle at last year's Christmas party,
the toilets had held a revelation for her when she overheard
a vitriolic Marilyn fuelled by cheap red wine. 'What kind of
man would fuck a skinny bitch like that, no hips, no tits, it
would be practically paedophilic.' When she was feeling
particularly virtuous Sumie tried to understand. Maybe
Marilyn was bitter that her own floppy udders and lumpy
ass never attracted any attention other than revulsion.
Nevertheless she hadn't gone so far as to forgive. It was the
two-facedness. The treachery of pretending to be one thing
when really you were the other. To her face Marilyn clucked
and simpered, as sweet as a Tootsie Roll but inside she was
rotten.
    Still Sumie nodded and agreed, smiled and didn't argue,
waited patiently for her to go away again.

Ah, good old Marilyn, always a kind word for my Susan.

You think you know what she is thinking, standing there
stewing in your own resentment. You hate her for her
slim, lithe figure, for her neat features. Even with none of
the make-up you cake your own face with she looks like a
harlot.

(Painted doll)

You don't trust her, the way she makes all the
men look at her, manipulates them into fawning over
her. Her quietness infuriates you – you know the
scheming, conniving nature it disguises. When she does
speak her stupid accent cannot help but grate along
the back of your neck, clanging your stomach muscles
together. You force yourself to smile, realising you are
in danger of drifting away in your ire. Knowing you
should feel superior but she always manages to
undermine you.

Susan must look to her as a surrogate mother, someone to explain the ropes. Marilyn's got a sensible head on her, she always made it subtly obvious how unsuitable she thought Alison was. If only I had listened to her then. She even offered to bring in some Tupperware dinners for me when she heard of the divorce.

You know Ted is looking over, his gaze causes your skin to prickle and your palms to sweat. How unfair it is that you are stuck upstairs after 'moving up in the company' while that little minx gets to be in the same room as Him. As soon as your message has been passed on you are banished again, back to the desk and misery which only belong to you.

Older women are always more considerate like that.

A quick glance at the neat watch around her wrist, bought with her very first American paycheck, and Sumie is relieved to see she doesn't have much longer to go. She spends so much time doing this she sometimes finds it hard to remember that there is a life outside of this ill-furnished box.

Tonight they will meet as they do every week, swapping homemade delicacies in Makio (Mary) and Jin's (James) shared apartment. Where they are all too scared to talk about the realities they were now confronted with daily. Instead they will reminisce about their Homes. Lives and customs that no longer have relevance. Things even the people who looked just the same couldn't fully relate to. They will get drunk on Southern Comfort wishing it were sake and discussed their own past situations and experiences as though they had all been there together, when really little of their past lives intersected. It was the comforting tongue that made a difference.

Makio was the only other woman at the gatherings, she was on the shrinking side of life with a frown/crease permanently etched between delicate pepper brows. Sumie couldn't help thinking she looked distinctly uncomfortable in her pink sweaters and department-store skirts. Although they live together as a couple Sumie suspects that Makio and Jin were not officially married. She would never ask them though, for risk of upsetting the balance. Sumie and Makio speak very carefully to each other.

She'll finish in half an hour. Let me help her on with her coat and give me that sweet little smile, murmuring that she hopes I have a nice evening. Knowing full well it would be much nicer if we were sharing it. Wish I could take her back with me right now, let her fill up all the spaces Alison left behind. She will make it smell good again, warm and welcoming. When I crack open a beer in front of the tube she will be there to make it taste all the sweeter.

It didn't bother Sumie that the female presence in the group was restricted to herself and Maiko; she felt unnaturally safe in the mainly male company. Sadness had diffused what would have once been a charged atmosphere.

The men themselves were humbled. The strength and power that had been so tangible in Japan was dwarfed and mocked in America. They were forced to fit inside itty-bitty roles that they couldn't avoid shrinking into. Often Sumie cried when she got back to her tiny apartment but the visits continued to be the highlight of her week.

Besides, most of them already had provincial wives. Still nurturing withering plans to save, save, save enough to bring them to the Golden World. Sumie thought maybe these hardworking and lonely women were actually better off where they were. Then again, she had eaten ice cream sodas, shopped in Sears. Just because she had quickly become cynical and derisive of these wonders didn't mean everyone would.

Sumie remembered her mother's shining eyes. Joy that her father's dream would come to fruition, but deep sadness that her daughter would be going somewhere she couldn't even imagine. The tiny cracked hands gripping her shoulders in an unusual outburst of affection. Sumie felt a roar of sadness and anger that they had been so mistaken.

Oh God, her cheeks are glowing a rosy pink, what can she be thinking? Does she know I am watching her? She looks like she has been exercising, exerting herself.

I will make her look like that every night. She will pleasure me long into the darkness.

(Blow-up doll)

Satisfied by my satisfaction, she will lie quietly beside me as we drift off to sleep.

Often she had nightmares. That she would be trapped here forever, that her Japanese papers would be destroyed and no one would believe where she truly belonged. That she would never see her family again, that her mother would die believing that she had stopped loving her. She would wake up in her cramped room, hearing all the wrong noises and smelling all the wrong smells. And know that something was fundamentally not right. Sometimes it would take her days to shake the fears away and assimilate to the way her life was now. She wondered if she was the only person who felt this way.

They had a saying over here: 'Home is where the heart is.' Sumie thinks that this is very true, and she knows where her own heart remains.

Soon I will ask her out. When I've heard a bit more about this partnership Brownlee was hinting at. When I'm sure Alison is firmly erased. When everything is perfect.

Her surprise will be exquisite, the joy brimming in her eyes, the knowledge she will always be safe with me almost too much for her to bear. It will be the last thing she expected but, quickly, she will see it is the only thing to do and throw herself into my arms. I'll finally be able to run my fingers through that waterfall of hair and squeeze that wonderfully proportioned body to mine.

Sumie comforts herself with thoughts of a future. She stands and glances around the room, searching for empty coffee cups so she can wash them like she is expected to even though it is not actually part of her job. Ted holds his out to her, poor guy, she knows he will always be stuck in this life. Ineffectual, bald and lonely.

Enough Dollars in her bank and she will be rich in Yen.

Sandra McQueen

MISFIT

We played dress-up;
paraded Mother's best frocks
in bridal trains
of trailing skirts
along the lino, waxed
to an inch of its life
so that
you could see
the pattern's faded lines, like
an old memory,
dull around the edges, but
with its purpose intact.

Our feet,
lost in shoes
already out of fashion,
as if promising that,
by growing into them, we would,
one day, revive their
elegant gait.

But, it wasn't
Father's clothes
we tried on
to test our wings.
We wore his opinions
and prejudices
the way we donned
Mother's clothes, glad
in the end, when
we outgrew them,
discarding them like
ill-fitting shoes.

Theresa Muñoz

GLASGOW SNOWFALL

wading through drifts
to reach the corner shop,
       snow
                (freezing my knees,
sticking me
to the street)
       falling as I come across
another soul
on the sidewalk's edge:

      a short snow-drunk

with a pebble mouth
and stick arms, offering up
a fist-crushed can
of Tennent's lager—

the bright red T, stark
against the sudden whiteness
in lazy March, flakes
stinging my chin

and the can tipping
slightly
       to the wind

toasting me (slowly
covered in white): a

good mornin!

Donald S. Murray

UNLIKELY RELATIONSHIPS

Emily Bronte and Nabokov
tumbled out of doors,
scrambling through snow,

While Collette became embroiled
in the life of Alfred Hitchcock,
spilling out of a rear window.

Catherine Cookson found herself
in a ditch
hitched up with Robert Burns

While Erica Jong was bound
to have cured her fear of flying,
clutching Biggles till daylight returned

And the Library Service discovered
both stripped and undercover,
secrets scattered wide and broad,

The most unlikely sets of lovers
the evening that the library van
skidded off the Sandwick Road.

Andrew Nicoll

THE COMPLETE WORKS

We were in a bar once, in Belgium it was, or Holland, I forget, and the wall was made of bits of broken, blue glass with water running down it, glistening and shining. We sat there in a row and drank that thick, yellow, floury beer until we were sick. God, all that money. Loading those fish at that wee pier in the middle of the night and all that money and no questions asked, no forms to fill in, no quotas, no log books, no nothing, just the money, just the vans driving away and the yellow lights that bounced into the dark and all that money and that bar with the blue wall.

I think about it all the time. When I'm on the deck and we're hauling nets and the stern dips down and the sea piles up behind in a shape like the back side of a spoon, curved out and up and higher than the radar mast. It makes me think of that wall in that bar.

I think about stuff like that a lot. It's because I hate the work. I hate it so much I can't say it. I just don't know how to say it. I haven't the words – and I'm a writer. I'm supposed to have the words. But I have been on this boat so long I forget everything.

Sometimes I am so tired I forget how to speak and it's been that way for years – since the school bell rang and I ran down the brae to freedom, never thinking I was running into a cage.

The boat was a cage. The work was a cage. As years went by even the sea became a cage that grew smaller with every tide and held me as close as the fish in the nets. When the sun shines it's like it's shining through the bars, clouds flicker across the sky like shadows at the window of my cell and the wind howls like it's whistling through a locked door.

That first trip out, when I couldn't stop smiling, they told me I'd soon learn. I didn't know what they were talking about. All I could see was the little grey town dipping away at the stern, half hidden by the winches and the black funnel-smoke and, maybe, if I listened awful hard, the electric clatter of the school bell. And I mistook it for a prison siren signalling an escape. I was out. I was away. But I had hurried into something worse.

It took me a while to find out and, somehow, when I did, it was worse for me than for the others. 'You'll get used to it,' they said. 'You'll learn.'

I learned, but I never got used to it. I never got used to the boat heaving under me or my guts heaving with it. I never got used to the nets coming aboard, bursting with struggling things, or the flapping. I can't stand the smells. I can't stand the diesel choke of it, the fish guts. It's everywhere. It brings the gulls that hang behind us like kites on a string. It's in the coffee. It's in my skin. Clothes that have never seen the sea stink of it. In the time it takes me to pick the pins out of a new shirt, the smell has woven itself into the cloth. And I can't get used to the pain. Freezing cold and soaking wet with little bits of salt and ice rubbing on your skin and your hand diving like an open beak and grabbing something that's still choking on a crumb of life. Hold it down, thumb in the eye. That bursting. That popping. Hold it down and slice. Drive the blade in and flick and open and there, those soft ropes of grey and blue and pink, the pearl colours of a spring dawn, all packed in and stored away as perfect as watch workings, grip them and tear. It's only a tug – enough to snag the skin at the arse end or wrench the tongue a little at the head end. I never get used to the pain.

Sometimes I dream that the whole boat is dragged under and then, when we are drowning and our lungs are bursting and the cold water is forcing its fingers between our lips, then the blades arrive and we open our mouths to scream but no sound comes. It's no more than we deserve.

Could we do it, any of us, if we could hear them cry? Maybe they could – the others. They none of them mind it like me. They call me strange – I know all about it. I know what they say. It doesn't matter. It never bothered me. It bothered me when I was a laddie and new on the boat and I wanted to be like them but I know now I am not like them and I'm glad of it.

I should never have come here. Some of us are born to be hewers of wood and drawers of water and move through life like cattle. I am not one of those. I am here by mistake. I should have had the sense to stay at the school. I see that now. But I fled from there like a prisoner on the run when all along they were offering me the keys to a different kind of jail. And now I can't get out.

So, what I do is, I make my prison beautiful. I am a writer and a poet and so that's what I do. I'm not like them. Standing there for hours, gutting fish, I write poems. I say them over and over in my head, sometimes the same line for hours at a time, dirling there like a toothache, until it sticks, until I've got it right. And then I write them down in a jotter.

They used to make fun of me.

One time we were steaming out to the grounds on a fine blue day with hardly a ripple and the sun sparking in off the water and nothing to do. We were all jammed in round the table drinking tea and eating bread and beans and Wee Alec reached under my pillow and grabbed my jotter – one of those dusty-green ones with two staples down the back. 'Fitdye dae wi' these? Aye scribblin'.'

He opened it up and held it over his head, like the work was written on the ceiling and he started reading one of my poems, swinging his arms about and clutching his chest and making sobbing faces. What a performance. Then they all joined in, holding my jotter high up and passing it round the table, taking turns to read a line or two and then flinging it on so it flew and fluttered round the galley. They were in the gang and I wasn't so they could mock me. It was allowed even when I belonged to the boat as much as any of them. But when I sat there and ate beans and drank tea and never stirred from my seat there was no fun in it for them so they stopped. Wee Alec had the jotter again. He spun it by a corner so it hit me softly in the chest and landed on the table. 'There,' he said, 'have it.'

After a while I said: 'They're no' a secret. It'll aa be published. I'm wanting a'body tae read them so you lads might as weel.'

They never bothered after that. Not once they saw I wasn't bothered. Sometimes they even said: 'You should write about that,' if something happened, like the regimental piper called to write tunes for remarkable events. Sometimes I do but they never looked in my jotters again.

There's a lot of them on the shelf next to the coffee can but they never read them. They just pile up there.

There are books you can get in the library that tell you

where to send your work. Books for authors. Places you can send work and have it printed. I used to send things all the time. I used to post off whole jotters and then, when I came back off the boat, they would be lying behind the door in an envelope that I'd addressed. Written to myself, by myself, for myself. One time I put a fiver between the pages. It was still there when the jotter came back. I don't send them now. I see now that's not the point. The work is the point. So nobody bothered and the jotters just piled up.

Nobody bothered until the day the laddie joined the boat. He looked like me – like I used to do – running out of school as fast as he could and glad to make the leap off the dock. And he had a job, money in his pocket to splash and that was more than most of the lads like him. There was something about him that made it hard not to punch him. Just the look he had, that skinny, white-faced look that laddies have when they're not wise enough to know that they don't know anything.

But he worked. We made sure he worked. He learned to work when he was asleep, the same as the rest of us, standing there and slashing through fish bellies and never heeding the cold and the salt in the cuts on his hands. One time he was standing next to me, grabbing and cutting and throwing and grabbing and looking at the wall and laughing. 'Look at the lampshades,' he said. 'I'll have to get seven of those for my mum.' It happens. It's happened to all of us. I worked the winch all night long once with a man in a fur coat sitting next to me. He turned out all right, the laddie.

One day I came into the cab and he was sitting there at the table with a jotter. He saw me and stuck it under the table, like I'd caught him with a dirty book – but there are piles of those around the place if he was wanting one. And then he saw there was no point pretending. 'Sorry,' he said.

'They're for readin',' I said.

'Shouldnae middle wi yir stuff.'

'They're for readin',' I said. 'Read it if yi want.'

He brought the jotter out from under the table. I made some tea and didn't watch him. His lips moved along the line. Bonny lad. I went out and leant on the rail and drank my tea and tried not to be sick.

The laddie never let on about the jotters but I looked at the pile. He'd read three of them. And that night, when we were standing together and gutting he said: 'I liked them.' I never let on. It's about the work. Write for the work, not for the reader.

The next day he read another one. The others made fun of him. Wee Alec blared at him. 'How are yi readin' that when yi could be readin' this?' and he opened the pages of a magazine with a woman spread over it like something you'd see on the floor in the ice-room. They all laughed and the laddie tried to smile but his ears were red under his hat.

'Fit did yi like?' I asked him that night. I was standing beside the winch when he walked past.

'I liked it aa. They're aa guid. Guid stories. Even the poems. An' ehdna much like poems.'

I pointed with my cigarette end to let him know he could go.

It was getting on for light when the nets came aboard and the laddie was shovelling fish down the chute when he said: 'That een aboot the drooned minister. I liked that fine.'

I'd forgotten all about it.

The laddie said: 'It made me think what it's like to get seek on a boat.'

I stopped shovelling. 'Yi ken fine fit it's like,' I said.

'Naah. Nivir seek me. Boats are rare things. Nivir been seek oan a boat.'

We turned for port the next day and, when we got in, the laddie went away home with the last of the jotters. 'I'll not lose them,' he said.

He didn't. He brought back every one of them – and a new one of his own with a picture of a yellow skateboard on the front of it. He sat at the table and wrote. Wee Alec looked at him and he looked at me and he looked back at the laddie but he never said a word. The whisky was still pounding in his head and he couldn't be bothered.

Later on, standing at the rail, ploughing straight for the sun, the laddie said: 'Jist if it's okay by you.'

'Fine.' I said.

'Yi dinna mind?'

'Nae bothered.'

'Nivir be's guid's you.'

'Have a shottie,' I said.

'Wid yi gies a hand?'

'I'd gie yi a hand.'

The laddie hardly said a word all that trip. Every minute he wasn't working he was writing in his book.

'Can I get tae see?' I said.

'Soon,' he said and he folded the jotter and put it in his pocket. He kept it there, wrapped in a plastic bag. Mine were all lying out by the coffee can and his was in his pocket.

We got paid on the harbour side and the laddie folded a lot of notes into a bundle and tucked them inside his coat. I said: 'Can I no' see yir stuff?'

'I'll bring it back,' he said. 'Honest. Read it then. It's no' din.'

I was waiting in the cab when he came back to the boat. Two days at home I'd thought of nothing else but the laddie's story and now he'd come back and I was ready for him. The work has to be shared. It dies on closed pages. It needs light and air and I would have to tell him that.

'Wid yi read this?' he said, 'Please? Yi said yi'd gie's a hand.' He held out a red plastic folder. 'I typed it up.'

I took the pages and flicked through them. There were twenty two. I said: 'Well, I've no time. I'll do whit I can.' I put the folder on the shelf on top of my jotters and I looked down at the table again.

'Aye, fine, fine,' he said. 'That's fine.'

I didn't read it all that day. I waited. The laddie deserved to wait. He looked at me while we were gutting fish. 'I'll read it,' I said. 'I'll read it.'

I read it secretly, the pages tucked inside my jacket and the folder left, empty, on the shelf. Nobody's business if I read it or not. But I read it.

It was wonderful. It was a story about a sailor who fished up pearls and wrote poems on them with a golden pin and threw them to the woman he loved whenever he passed the lighthouse where she lived. They never met, they never spoke, but she loved him for his poems and she wore them on a necklace all her days. It was wonderful. And the sea in it was beautiful and wide and open and the gulls were happy and the sun shone and the stars sparkled.

'It's rubbish,' I said. 'Sorry but it's jist nae guid. Well, for a first attempt, it's maybe no aa that bad.'

'Naa, it's rubbish,' the laddie said. 'I'll no bother.'

I was the only one that saw him go to the back of the boat and throw it over. Every page turned into a seagull and flew away, white and screaming.

Tom Pow

SELKIE

It was around the first time I recall
seal culls had featured on the evening news.
After tea, from deep in our couch, we'd watched
giant figures, padded like hockey stars

take their clubs onto the ice. The seal cubs'
mothers, at a distance, tipped back their heads—
their cries were almost human. The men dragged
the pelts, writing their blood into the snow.

Mum looked at the sealskin gloves where they lay,
still on their Christmas paper, in the sheen
of the tree lights, and in spite of our Dad's
'Aye, they'll keep you warm, Agnes' glow, she knew

these gloves would never leave the house again
while she lived. Wary of the risk, she said,
'someone might hack my hands off at the wrists.'
For hadn't she seen in the same news item,

as well as the calm killers, the close ups
of the cull protestors too, their red eyes
fiery for justice? But at the least,
she acknowledged, Dad hadn't short-changed her—

misguidedly perhaps, he'd bought her the best.
She pulled them on and held them before her,
smiling, for my father. Her fingers were still,
the gloves clumsy, out of their element.

Each was a small pelt in itself; silver
and precious as it caught and shed the light.
They bore a glint of underwater ice
from that other world around their edges.

*

I never saw her wear the gloves again,
but from time to time, if visitors called,
she'd take them from the drawer they lived in—
buried beneath scarves, stoles and innocent

wearable gloves – like a secret to be shared.
They'd sit then on her lap and she'd stroke them
in the way that fisherwomen would care,
in selkie stories, for a baby seal

they'd saved from the cruel workaday world,
lifting it from the darkness when they could
and feeding it with snatches of sunlight.
At the end of such stories, it's understood

the grown seal finds its way home to the sea
and may even take the woman with it.
No longer human now like you or me,
she'll live on beneath the foam; though at times

you may glimpse a familiar old grey head
bobbing in the water and think you see,
from far out, a glistening fin wave—
before the seal dives back into the grave.

Heather Reid

DISCOMBOBULATING

We discovered the word in Spain,
cockily stretched across the sleeve of
a holiday read, some critic showing off
or perhaps we were just thick
(four degrees between us and we hadn't got a clue).
Still we liked its style, its pace, its jizz,
the elasticity of its nature,
the bob, bob, bobbing alongness of
its arrangement and the endless possibilities
of words it could spawn.

It became a kind of mantra,
thrown like a grenade into conversations
and rattled around mouths like a boiled sweet
until our tongues furred with its familiarity.
We exposed it in bars and restaurants,
like a webbed foot or a two-headed sheep,
and whispered its soothing vowels
beneath the discombobulating stars
of a Spanish night sky.

In time we grew tired of its jaunty
disposition and lowered its tone, smearing
its reputation into a fudge of smut and innuendo,
until finally its flaccid form drew scorn.
Back in Britain we introduced it to our youngest son,
packed it into his head like some exotic fruit
and sent him off to school (go impress your teacher, we said)
only to find him later, huffy in his room,
reprimanded in class for trying to be smart.

Alan Riach

THE MOTHER SPEAKS TO HER SON

When you come home from the city to your village
you tell me nothing about where you live now.
Your clothes must be different there. You are wearing
the old style here. But things seem changed somehow.

The buffalo walk by the river as usual
and the mist suffuses the valley as the tea crops
surround the slopes on the terraces. This is normal.
Your eyes return to the road outside the gate, and to the
    mountain-tops.

You walk among your people once again at the turn of the
    year
and you will not speak to me of your life away from here.
The light in your eyes this morning smooths yesterday's
    lines from your brow.
And my love is undiminished, though you are a stranger to
    me now.

Dilys Rose

MAD HATTER SYNDROME

It wasn't only carroting furs
or steaming felt hats into shape
which made his hair and teeth fall out
and caused him to mumble and lurch
through town, leaning on an empty pram;
it wasn't only the mercury fumes
seeping through his skin and lungs;
it wasn't only that he had to mask
his symptoms or be out of a job,
or that he needed clean air and sunshine
but couldn't take the time off work;
it wasn't only that fashion demanded
a man of the moment must wear a hat—
it was also lying awake at night,
seeing the slow cortège of forebears
tremble through his own delirium
and knowing that raving jitter
of wage slaves was his only inheritance.

Hester Ross

SELF-PORTRAIT

The shallow water on the shores of Lake Malawi is the worst place, absolutely the worst place, for bilharzia: the tiny snails that get in through paddling feet and work their way up, all the way up, destroying the vital organs. You can't worry about these things – you'd go mad. Just face the facts: Africa's a dangerous place. And, as a mother, you have to take precautions. That's really all you can do to keep the tides of fear at bay.

The lake's out of bounds then, so, to get the shot I want: 'Boys with boat behind,' I line up the three of them – under protest – in front of the hotel pool with the good ship *MV Kingfisher* in the background. I crouch right down so that through the lens you can't make out the strip of sand between the pool and the infected lake with the boat on it – and the effect is quite good. A *trompe l'oeil* they call it – something that deceives the eye.

The boys banter and bicker as usual and are too big and noisy even for this Boxing Day pool filled with laughter and splashing and high-spirited squeals. At one point they manage to fall together in a heap into the deep end and emerge wet and laughing and fully clothed. Enough. I'm exhausted. The wet shot is, I suspect, the best of the twenty or so I've taken – I've gone digital, you see. I only want one, just one good photo, to add to my collection. One more piece of evidence in defence of their happy boyhood; a great holiday: 'Safe arrival at Nkudzi Bay, 26th December 2005, on *MV Kingfisher* following wonderful – wonderful – Christmas sail to Liwonde game park.'

But still, the boys have been cooped up for two days on the boat – sorry, 'ship', as the captain calls it. He brought it with him all the way from Kariba 25 years ago, he says, after they lost the war. Quite.

And now, the pool is just too busy for serious swimming. No letting off steam here. Table tennis? Golf? There should just be time before nightfall for a few holes with their father on the hotel's nine-hole course. Let them work off their endless adolescent energy: stretch their long and growing limbs. No wonder I'm done-in. I'll go back to the rondavel to shower and change: find just a little space. We agree to meet up by the pool in half an hour? Maybe it will be quieter then and I'll have that well-earned sundowner as they swim.

*

'An African boy,' says the woman.
'A child?'
She nods.
I have noticed that many of the younger Asian women now wear cropped trousers and t-shirts but this lady sits alone at one of the wrought-iron tables in yards of pale blue nylon. I've just showered but already I am sweating in the heavy damp air. She looks cool and I hover beside the empty chairs. I guess her husband has joined the small crowd round the child. We speak in whispers as the noisy chatter of the holiday, the screams of delight from the kids in the pool, have hushed to silence. A few – too many – of the holiday-makers have gone to watch the attempts at resuscitation and the rest have disappeared, taking their children right away.
They thought, the woman tells me, that the child had lain at the bottom of the pool for at least fifteen minutes, maybe longer.
'The lifeguards didn't notice?'
'There are no lifeguards here.'
I had arrived to see people moving to a spot at the side of the pool towards the deep end. Now, I scan the tangle of limbs of the crowd but can't make out the centre of their attention. There is no sign of my boys.
'I came to find my children,' I say.
'It was an African,' she repeats. She turns away.
'I'm sorry, I'm intruding.'
'No,' she sniffs into her paper napkin. 'Not at all, I'm just upset. Sit down.'
She asks me where I've come from. I tell her we used to live in Zomba and we're on a return visit. Have I noticed much change? A bit, I say. Everything is going down, she says, the security is now terrible. I say I'd noticed Blantyre has changed. The shops I knew have moved. The Central Bookshop. Faida's the hairdresser. I name two prominent Asian businesses. Everyone knows the Sacranies.
Yes, she says, they've all moved to the big out-of-town shopping centre. It is better there, parking is secure and a

guard at the barrier keeps out local vendors. She says this with approval. Her husband too is a businessman. Do I know her husband's company? General Refrigeration.

'Yes,' I say. We had bought our fridge there when we'd first arrived. I remembered the name.

'And I too have a business,' she says. 'It's so much better than sitting at home with nothing to do all day.'

The group opposite starts to break up. Somebody is moving a wooden sun-lounger forward. We watch as the boy is carried away from the pool. It is the first time we have seen him. He lies stretched out on his side. A boy of about ten or eleven. Orange trunks and slender brown legs.

The woman dabs her eyes and shakes her head. We sit in silence for some moments.

'I have a toilet roll factory. There was a gap in the market,' she says.

'Oh really.' I hear the words: *breathing now* but also *no chance*.

'Not the cheap thin kind,' she says. 'First quality. Like this,' she says, thrusting towards me the thick paper napkin she had wiped her tears with. 'You want some? I'm doing export.'

*

Next morning the pool is empty. My husband says it's awkward. It would be good to have a last swim before breakfast, but we should show respect. Then we notice the signs saying 'Under treatment.' Hannes has appeared – not Captain Hannes now – and directs the pool attendants in roping off the deep end. He comes to greet us.

'Did the child die?' I ask him as his wife joins us.

'Yes,' he says. 'It happens.'

'The lifeguards didn't see him? They say he was there for fifteen minutes.'

'You can't have lifeguards here,' says Hannes. I fail to ask *why not*. 'Nobody saw him. The place was full of people. Boxing Day. Nobody saw him. I've told the pool attendants not to beat themselves up. They've taken five people out alive in the last six months. If you lose one …'

'Nobody saw him.'

'The family wanted to use the beach,' explains his blonde wife. She's a big-boned woman – too big, I think, for her

sprigged and frilly girlish shift − and she talks with the
clipped vowels and hard emphatic consonants of an African
colonial. She could have come from anywhere between
Kenya and the Cape. You often find such people drafted in
to places like this. To sort things out. Get things running.
Put the books straight.

'I told them that's okay, but if they wanted to go into
the pool they had to ask me first.' She means that non-
residents had to pay. The boy had been trespassing. The hotel
can not be blamed.

My boys arrive for breakfast and Hannes gives them five.
It was a great sail, we say. An unforgettable Christmas. We
apologise to Mrs Hannes for taking her husband away on
Christmas day.

'Ach,' she says. 'That's how he likes it. He likes to get
into the bush.'

Families are leaving at the end of the holiday weekend.
Porters wheel luggage from rondavels past the empty pool
towards the reception. New guests will arrive this afternoon.
They'll take away the ropes and they'll open up the pool.

I sit in the shade of a big cedrela tree and scroll through
the pictures on the camera. It saves time to delete the rejects
right away. There are a couple of shots which look okay.
But the one with the boys dripping might well be the best. I
zoom in to check for closed eyes or odd expressions. To
the right of my youngest son there is a blur of orange. I
zoom out. I hadn't noticed a boy diving into the pool. I look
at the next few shots.

My boys are pulling silly faces and in every frame there
is a dark shadow in the blue of the water.

Cherise Saywell

GHOST TRAIN

I saw it first, but I didn't touch it. Roy did. Standing over it
with a long stick, he prodded it gently and although we had
thought it was dead it raised its head and snarled. Its teeth
were coated with something slimy, and its tail and rump
were flattened so that you couldn't tell what was mangy fur
and what was the red dirt it was lying on. There were already
maggots on it.

'Been hit by something,' Roy said.

'Ghost train, maybe,' I replied, pushing my foot against
a length of rusted metal and looking along the rough empty
bend of track. There hadn't been trains here since before we
were born. From where I was standing you could see up to
the new line. You had to climb a steep rocky embankment to
cross it but even there I'd never had to stop for a train. They
mostly came through our town at night.

Roy poked at the fox and the flies rose from it like dust
off a rug. He liked examining things. He'd turn over the
corpse of a rabbit, or pick through the remnants of a bird's
nest, just to see what else he could make of it. Most of the
stuff you saw down here was dead, nearly always cats or
rabbits. They were usually closer to the new tracks and you
could tell most of them had been knocked by trains. I'd even
seen a wallaby once, a female. Her nipples were swollen
but her pouch was empty and there was blood in her ears.

I shuffled back. There was no way the fox could get near
me in the state it was in, but the noise coming from it made
me nervous. I sat down at a safe distance and stretched my
legs out in front of me. They were newly shaven and I
couldn't stop thinking about how different I felt. When the
hairs were there the wind would tickle against them. Now
the skin felt deliciously numb. Roy hadn't noticed yet. He
was still bent over the fox which was growling for all its
remaining worth. It was strange how it didn't sound
wounded, even though there couldn't be much life left in it.

'Leave it be, Roy,' I said, 'It's near dead anyway. Don't
tease it.'

'I'm not hurting it, just trying to see if it can get up.'

I didn't reply because it was obvious the fox wasn't going

to walk anywhere again in this life. I got up and began to pick my way along the sleepers, balancing on the rails where the wooden beams were buried. 'C'mon, Roy,' I called back.

He dropped the stick beside the fox and I let him overtake me so I could look at his back, how it had broadened and how muscled his arms were in their t-shirt. At the beginning of the summer he'd shorn his hair. It was pelt-sleek, hardening the planes of his face. He had girlfriends now too, mostly with dyed blonde hair. Their ears were pierced in two or three places and they wore makeup to school. But we'd still plan to meet up occasionally, somewhere along the old line, and then we'd walk to the carriage that stood where the yards had once been.

I was thinking about the fox again by the time we got there.

'D'you think a dog got it?' I asked Roy. 'One of those greyhounds of Jack Torpy's? He walks them down here sometimes.'

'Maybe.'

'Or it might've got hit by a car and dragged itself here.'

'Not with its back legs like that. Did you see 'em?'

'They were practically gone.'

'I know.'

Roy peered in through a small window to make sure we were our own. For a long time someone had lived in the carriage. Then, there were curtains on all the windows and through the chinks you could see a camping stove, a kettle, a set of drawers, an ashtray. Now it was a shell, leaking water and bleeding rust.

Inside, the air was thick and musty and the walls were mottled with mould. A weed grew down through the ceiling, its leaves pressed against the windows as though the carriage was moving and there was a view to see. We kept a cut of carpet to sit on; I could feel its damp weave through my shorts.

'What've you got?'

Roy swung his knapsack off his shoulder and squatted opposite me.

'Fags.' He put a magazine down between us, and laid the cigarettes on it.

'Whose?'

'His.' He counted them out. One was bent but the others were in good nick.

'What kind are they?'

'Crap. Peter Jackson. But at least they're not menthol.'

'Your mum still smoke menthol?'

'No. She smokes his.' Roy picked up one of the cigarettes and put it down again.

'He around for a while then?' I asked.

He shrugged. 'Dunno.'

Roy's mum had a new boyfriend. He was called Puss and I'd been trying to think of the reasons why a man might be called that. I saw him once, and he made me think of Puss in Boots. He had a smooth look, with his hair combed back and a neat moustache. But he was drunk and swaying and looked at me in a way that made me wish I'd worn a longer skirt.

'Why do they call him ... ?' The words were away before I could stop them. I pushed at the cuticles of my thumbnail and waited for something to swallow the silence. Roy divided the cigarettes, giving me the bent one.

'What've you got then?' he asked.

I pulled out a bottle.

'Geez.' Roy didn't try to hide that he was impressed. Usually I just brought Coca Cola or Fanta.

I peered through the green glass. 'It's red,' I said.

'Where'd you get it?' he asked.

'Mum got it from someone at work.'

'Does she know where it's gone?'

' 'Course not.'

He ran his hand down the side of the bottle. 'Got an opener?'

'Uh huh.' I retrieved it and laid it down between us.

'Do you like wine then?'

'No.'

'Me neither.' He sat back and pressed his hands against his thighs. 'Doesn't matter.'

'But look,' I said, 'I brought this.' I pulled a plastic bottle from my bag. 'Raspberry cordial. To make it sweet.'

Roy pressed his forefinger against his top lip and grinned at me. 'Thought of everything, haven't you?' He opened the bottle and I collected the two cups we kept with our carriage stuff. I poured a measure of cordial into each and then filled them up with wine.

'She'll notice this is gone,' Roy said.

'I know.'

'What'll you tell her?'

I rested my hands on my new smooth knees. 'I haven't decided yet. I'll worry about that when it happens.' I picked up the bent cigarette and then put it down again and took one that was undamaged. Roy leaned in and lit it for me. I dragged deep and felt the cheap punch in my lungs.

'Here.' Roy took it from me and blew a smoke ring. One of his eyes watered and he squinted it. Then he passed it back to me and gathered all the unsmoked ones into the middle of the magazine. 'We'll just share 'em, eh?'

I smiled. I could feel the damp imprint from his lips on the end of the cigarette. My head was spinning. The only time I ever smoked was when I came here with Roy and inhaling always made me feel light-headed.

'Y'know, Roy,' I said, blinking hard to slow the spinning sensation, 'there are horses in the paddock on the other side of the tracks.'

'Yeah, so?'

'So maybe it got trampled.'

'What?'

'The fox. Maybe it got trampled by a horse.'

Roy shrugged. 'Doesn't matter now, does it? And anyway, foxes are vermin.'

'Are they?'

'Yup.'

I took another puff and passed the fag to Roy. 'Perhaps we should take it some water,' I suggested.

'It can't even get up,' he said. 'How's it going to drink water?'

'We could pour it on its snout. Some would go in its mouth, if we did it carefully.'

'Don't know if I want to get that close to it though.' He took a slug of the red drink. 'This is nice, like this. Sweet. Doesn't taste like wine at all.'

I grinned and sipped at mine. I was already beginning to feel a little tipsy so I put it down and leaned back, stretched my legs out.

Roy's eyes moved with me. 'New legs,' he said, and ran

a hand lightly along my skin. We'd been friends for so long, it had always been okay for us to touch. But now, without hair on my legs, I felt naked.

'When did you do this?' he asked without looking up.

'Yesterday.'

'Your old lady noticed?'

'Not yet.'

'You'll get a row when she does though.'

'Yeah. But I'm old enough now. Don't you reckon?'

'Yeah. 'Course.'

I swallowed, searching for the right thing to say. 'You like it?'

'Mmmm. Smooth.'

Roy's hand was still on my leg. His skin was brown and unblemished and the bones of his wrists jutted out a little. He ran his fingers along my shin, then tucked them behind my knee. I wondered if I was sweaty there and drew my legs away, gulping at my raspberry wine to disguise the awkwardness of the moment.

Roy dragged on the last of his cigarette, stubbed it out on the floor, and poured himself some more wine. He didn't sweeten it with the cordial this time.

'This carpet's filthy,' I said, upturning my palms and examining the grit and dirt embedded there.

'Hmmm.' Roy stared out the window. Its glass pane was intact but it was thick with scum and I couldn't tell what he was seeing. I didn't want him to be moody with me and I cast about in my head for something to do, something to say that would get us back to how we'd always been without erasing whatever had just happened.

Eventually, I stretched my legs out again, tentatively.

'Imagine if this was part of a moving train,' I said.

Roy put his drink down and looked at me.

'If this carriage was attached to a moving engine and you could go anywhere, where would you go?' I asked him.

He rolled the unsmoked cigarettes back and forth beneath two of his fingers.

'Dunno.'

'No. C'mon,' I coaxed. 'There must be somewhere.'

'I like it here. I wouldn't go anywhere. I'd do it up and live in it.'

He took another cigarette and lit it. When the match

went out he drew it across in front of his face. You could smell the sulphur. 'I love that smell,' he said.

'Me too.'

'Why? Is there somewhere you'd go?' he asked.

'Yeah, I guess. Nowhere specific. But a city, definitely.'

Roy was surprised. 'Why?'

'The lights, I suppose,' I said. I tipped my head to one side and tried to appear careless. 'At night. And things happening all the time. You could be alone and still feel like part of something. Cities are ...' I had to search for the right words because I only knew about quiet streets with grassed gutters and roads with potholes you could swerve your bike around without even looking. There was no brightness, no neon, no traffic lights. 'If you look at a picture of a city,' I said, 'it's a crowd of shapes and colours and ... places to hide, I guess.'

I'd been looking at the scummy window, trying to say what I thought, but when I turned back Roy wasn't listening. He was blowing smoke rings. With his head tipped back he puffed perfect circles that shimmered a little against the filthy backdrop and then faded. I watched his throat and the muscles at the side of his neck. He blew a final smoke ring and then handed the cigarette to me.

'Go on. You try.'

'I can't do smoke rings.'

'Just try.'

I drew on the cigarette but choked and coughed a rough cloud of smoke and spit.

'That's not very good,' Roy said, and laughed. I laughed too and tried again but I couldn't work out what to do with my tongue to make the little circles.

Roy leaned over, took the cigarette from me and then pressed a kiss to my lips. I tasted sugar and wine, nicotine and skin. The mix was intoxicating and my head was full of bubbles. I closed my eyes and saw myself living with Roy, here in the carriage, with a bed under the window where the weed was, and the walls painted butter yellow. I'd put curtains up, and a proper rug on the floor. The windows would be clean and we would be able to see everything. But when Roy ran his hand against my newly shaved legs I got to thinking of my mum and what she'd say when she noticed them. Then I thought about Roy's mum and her boyfriends, how long the nights would be, waiting for someone to come home with just the breeze outside and the occasional train going by in the distance.

I pulled away and took a gulp of my drink. 'Geez, my mouth feels dry,' I said. 'I really need a drink of water.'

Roy re-lit his fag and smoked it down in silence. Then he said, 'We should go. I've got to be somewhere.'

We hid the rest of the wine and the cordial and collected the cigarettes.

'Go on, you can have them,' I offered. 'I only smoke here anyway.'

He slipped them into his chest pocket. 'Yeah. Thanks,' he said. 'I'll buy some next time. So we've got decent ones to smoke.'

Outside it was getting dark. You couldn't see stars yet but they were there, waiting behind the curtain of dusk. We walked quickly along the tracks, and by the time we got to where the fox had been the light was dull and grey. I could barely see its outline now. We only paused for a moment. Roy didn't touch it this time. There was silence and a leaden stillness around it and I knew it was dead. I struck out ahead of Roy and he didn't try to pass me. I listened to rocks crunching under our feet. Then, to break the silence, I said, 'That fox. I reckon it got knocked from up there.' I pointed towards the new tracks.

'No way,' Roy said. 'Too far.'

But I thought about how small the fox was, how neat and light, and how a night train might toss it like a stone skimmed along the surface of a lake.

Alexis Scott

MARTIN
(Novel Extract)

I wis half-expectin him. Cags. Eyewis turns up whenever I start thinkin aboot him. When I'm tryin *no* tae think aboot him. Plus it wis knockin on for midnight an Cags eyewis kept late oors. In fact it wis early for Cags, so it wis.

In the windae again. This is gettin ridiculous.

He's barely in two minutes when there's a knock at the door. It'll be that Johnson wifie, I wis thinkin. She'll've seen him climbin in for sure an I'll be gettin threw oot on my neck. So much for learnin tae make soup.

Only it wis Tracy.

I thought I heard ye still up. I wis goinae hae a smoke, she says, I wis wonderin if ye wanted tae come wi us for a walk roon the block.

Aye, well, I says, hesitatin cause I wasnae sure aboot leavin Cags there hissel. I mean, he's my pal an aw that but he can be a bit light-fingered, especially when he's desperate and lately I only seem tae see him when he's desperate. No that I've much tae steal but I've a wee personal stereo an an alarm clock so they must be worth somethin. Plus me claes, I suppose.

Cags gied the game away hissel. He coughed. Bloody awful cough as a matter o fact.

Tracy kent straightaway.

Oh, didnae realise ye had company. Pardon me for interruptin.

It's okay, jist come in, I says.

I'm desperate for a fag but.

Aw right then, I says. But can we no jist go tae the door?

So we jist went tae the door an smoked oor fags.

I hate comin here an smokin on my ain, Tracy says.

Aye, so dae I.

So, he's a pal o yours, right?

Aye, sorta.

Whit dae ye mean, sorta? Ye dinnae ken if he's a pal or no?

Aye. That's aboot it.

I ken whit ye mean, she says then. I'm the same. Only right now I dinnae hae any pals. Except maybe you.

Maybe?

She smiled then. Well, except you then.

Maybe I can come and make ye soup when ye get your flat?

You'll be gettin a place as well, won't you?

Aye, well, it's no guaranteed but.

Whit aboot your pal?

Whit aboot him?

Where does he stay?

He doesnae. Jist comes an crashes at mine sometimes. Only dinnae say onything tae Ma Johnson or I'll get booted oot.

Course not. Christ, but, is he on the street?

Aye, some o the time.

That's terrible. Christ, I thought we were bad, stuck in this place.

Aye, it's no that bad, is it?

Sometimes I wish I could stay here. I'm no that bothered for gettin a hoose.

Me neither. I suppose we'd get sick o Ma Johnson eventually but.

Aye, eventually.

Ye couldnae really stay here wi a wean but, could ye?

I dunno. I wis thinkin, actually, maybe it'd be harder for them tae pit us oot wi a wean.

Aye, but they'll definitely gie you a hoose.

Ye think so?

Aye, sure they wull.

Sometimes I think it'd be great havin my ain place. Then there's other times I can see mysel climbin the walls. Goin aff my heid, like, bein on my ain all the time. Plus wi the wean it might be worse. I ken fuck all aboot how tae bring up weans.

Did ye no hae any brothers or sisters?

Aye, but we were separated, like, when I wis in care.

Aye, right. Me as well.

Aye. When you're in care everybody's eye tellin ye tae dae this an dae that. Ye think eftir ye leave ye'll hae your ain freedom an that but ye dinnae. Like, noo everybody's eyewis tellin me tae stop smokin as well.

Because you're pregnant?

Aye. The doctors say it'll make the baby wee. I dinnae mind it bein wee but. It might make it easier.

Are you feart o haein it, like?

Christ, aye, I'm feart. I want them tae put me oot, like, get wan o they Caesarians but they says they dinnae dae them routine, like.

Ye'd hae a big slit in your stomach, then, but.

Aye, I ken, Christ. Cannae win, eh? So, is your pal goinae stay wi you the night?

Aye, I suppose so. The trouble is, sometimes when I let him stay I cannae get rid o him.

Maybe Ma Johnson wid let him stay if we asked her nicely.

Aye, that'd be right.

What's he called?

Cags, short for Charlie.

Charlie's short for Charles.

Well, I dunno. That's what he says. He's aw right, Cags, I suppose. He's my best pal, really. Thing is, but, when I dae let him stay it can be awfy hard tae get rid o him. I mean, I like haein my ain room tae.

Whit aboot Mrs Forsyth's room?

Well, her stuff's still in it, but.

Aye, but she's away, isn't she?

I dunno.

She's probably no really drooned in the river. I mean, they'd've fun her by noo, wouldn't they?

Aye, maybe.

And even if she is, it's no as if it's oor fault. It's a good room goin tae waste when there's a hameless person could be daein wi it.

Aye, that's true. But it's locked onyway.

Aye, but Johnson's got the key.

She wouldnae gie it to us, but, would she?

Naw, I doot it. But maybe we could break intae her flat an jist take it.

Have you done this sorta thing before?

Naw. Have you?

Aye, a few times. I got caught but. I'm shite at it and I dinnae want tae be in trouble wi the law again.

Aye, but even if we got caught Johnson wouldnae clipe. She's no that bad.

Ye reckon?

Aye. Listen, this is whit we'll dae. She'll be blootered oot her brain the night. She eyewis is by this time o night. I'll go and knock an see if she answers. If she doesnae answer it means she's oot for the coont, right? Ye can jist tak a crowbar tae the door an go in an get the keys.

I've never used a crowbar before. My pal Cags has but.

Has he?

Maybe we could jist use the crowbar tae get intae Mrs Forsyth's room. Then we wouldnae need tae disturb Johnson at aw.

Other folk'd maybe hear us but. Like the new guy, Pete. His room's jist next door, ken.

Unless we got him in on it.

He might clipe but.

D'ye think he looks the type but?

Dunno. Cannae eyewis tell.

I'm freezin. Will we go in?

Wait a minute. The rain's goin aff. Let's take a walk roon the back.

I nearly jist said, Naw, Tracy. I cannae be bothered. There wis mair things I coulda said but didnae. Like, we were jist bein daft, weren't we, talkin aboot breakin intae Mrs Johnson's flat an then talkin aboot breakin intae Mrs Forsyth's room. Maybe if the two o us had been callin them Mrs instead o the auld this and the auld that all alang we'd never've contemplated daein onythin daft because, well, because, ye dinnae dae daft things tae folk ye respect, tae your friends, dae ye? Only it's only when ye're wi your friends that ye dae end up daein daft things. Or I dae, onyway. Noo it doesnae sound that daft takin a walk roon the back, no when it wis jist drizzlin and we'd jist been discussin breakin in. I tell mysel noo I wis goinae say tae Tracy that I jist wanted tae forget it, that it wis all daft talk when she hud the baby tae think aboot and the two o us had oor lives aheid o us and it wisnae oor fault Cags had fucked his life up before it started. And I wis very likely on the point o jist tellin her aw this when we reached my room an peeked in and there wis Cags, lyin, flaked oot, on the bed.

I can see whit ye mean aboot it bein awfy hard tae get rid o him, Tracy says. He's no exactly capable o walkin oot the door, is he?

I shook my heid. Then I saw it. I mean, I cannae help whit I see wi ma ain eyes, can I?

I walked towards Forsyth's windae and pointed, slowly. Whit?

It's Mrs Forsyth's room, I whispered.

Aye, well, so. Oh, fuck, I see whit ye mean. *Fuck.*

The windae wasnae even shut. It wisnae wide open but it was definitely open. It mighta jist been a crack but a crack is open. And an open windae is nae bother tae get intae. Ye might say it wis temptation but we musta thought it wis Providence. Okay, lookin back I can see it wis stupid, because it wisnae as if a coupla nights in a hostel wis goinae spell the end o aw Cags's problems. It wisnae as if we had fun this wondrous squat for him, that he could keep till the court flung him oot or whitever. It wis jist a bit o a kid-on, I suppose, and right then me an Tracy needed a kid-on. Or maybe I jist needed Tracy tae think I wis someone brave, maybe for the first time in my life I needed a lassie tae look up tae me, tae think I wis good at somethin. Because up till then I'd spent my hale life wi folk takin the mickey oot us, folk thinkin I wis an eejit jist cause I get epileptic fits.

Tracy gied us a shove and then I wis on the windowsill. I couldnae see a thing inside because the curtains wis drawn. But I stretched up and put my hand tae the latch and it wis dead easy, openin it wide. Only maybe no so easy tae climb through it. It wisnae that the gap wis that big, jist that it wis goinae be a bit o a leap and I'm no really a leapin sort o person. When it came tae PE at oor school I eyewis skived, ken. No leapin aboot or ony o they acrobatics for me.

Look, Tracy goes, dead calm and collected (well, she wisnae the wan goinae huvin tae be daein the leapin and divin – no wi a bump thon size), Look, Martin, jist haud the top pairt o the windae open and shove your heid an shoulders in. Then I'll lift up your legs and gie you a push an that'll be it.

Maybe I shoulda turned roon and says, Look, Tracy, dinnae be daft, you're six month up the pole, for Christ's sakes. Ye cannae go liftin the likes o me, even if I am a nine stone weaklin. Ye'll miscarry or somethin. Instead I kept my mooth shut an did as I wis telt, maybe because Tracy has that kinda effect on people and maybe also because I wisnae goinae object tae a wee shove frae Tracy. Even before she reached up and gied us a big shove on the arse I could feel this stirrin in my boxers.

The next minute I wis in the air an, I huvnae a clue till this day how she managed it but then I wis in the room. I wis inside an Tracy wis ootside. The place wis pitch black but I wis feart tae put on the light in case Johnson or Peter or somebody came alang and realised somebody wis where they shouldnae be. Mighta phoned the polis for aw I kent. Instead I reached and drew back the curtains but there wis hardly ony light in the sky, o course, by this time so it didnae make a lot o difference.

The room wis actually a bit pongy which surprised me as Forsyth didnae seem the type. It shows you wi auld biddies but, I says tae mysel. I didnae want tae linger ony longer than wis necessary onyway. Simplest thing tae dae, I thought, wid be tae get tae the door an open it an let Tracy in. Tracy wid ken whit tae dae, how tae keep the door open, ken.

Somebody wis approachin. For a minute I thought it wis Tracy but then I heard her ootside.

Martin, Martin, are ye there?

Somebody wis puttin the fuckin key in the fuckin lock. I ran to the windae an shut it. Then I climbed intae the wardrobe but I couldnae quite shut the door. Jist as well – I didnae want tae be locked in.

The person that came in put the light on an shut the door. I assumed it wis Forsyth. She'd been on a bender, I telt mysel. They were aw the same, these auld biddies, wan minute giein you shite aboot the dangers o drugs an the next minute blootered oot their brains.

Christ. Jesus fuckin Christ, I heard the voice say. I knew then who it wis. The Irish guy. The dour bastard that widnae gie ye the time o day. Probably in the Real IRA or something. No way wis I goinae come oot the wardrobe wi a mad bastard like thon.

Then I heard these snufflin sounds. I realised he wis cryin. Maybe he didnae realise he wis in the wrang room. Maybe he wis an alkie an all. I wis beginnin tae realise how many alkies there wis in a place like this an this yin wasnae even auld. In fact he didnae look much aulder n me.

Next thing I sees this great cardboard box and he goes ower tae the bed an I hear aw these noises. I'm wonderin if I could jist sneak past him an even if he sees us, so fuckin what because what the fuck is he doin here onyway? Only I'm too fuckin cowardly, too yella, they used tae say at the school. Shitey-pants Martin, some o the nastier wans said. No that I've done that in years. Even when I took a fit I never shat mysel, jist pissed ma troosers.

I wisnae shittin mysel in Forsyth's wardrobe but I wisnae that far aff it. I mean, I wis eye up tae high doh onyway – I hadnae exactly settled intae the place because there wis tae much comins and goins aw the time. Tracy and me were the only wans tae stay ony length o time. Naebody else ever stayed lang enough tae ken them, that wis the lang an the short o it.

I probably never wida hud the nerve tae make for the door. I mean, even if he had nothin tae dae wi the IRA he wis still a tough-lookin bastard. Coulda made mincemeat oota me in nae time. Still, if I had any idea he wis going onywhere near the wardrobe I woulda been oota there like a shot. Done a runner. I can dae it when I try. I'd a definitely tried it. I mean, I cannae run, runnin gies me asthma, but for Jesus' sake if I'd a kent he was goin onywhere near the bloody wardrobe, as I say.

What the fuck? What in the name o fuck are you doin in thur, you miserable wee piece o shite?

Dinnae get me wrang, dinnae think for a minute I'm ower-sensitive aboot folk swearin. It isnae that, I swear tae Christ. Even though I wis brought up in a hame an there wis wan guy there that wance threatened tae break every bone in my body if he heard anither swear word oota me, even though I've been battered tae fuck mony's the time fir it, I ken fine that folk swear, that swearin is a normal thing tae dae in the twenty-first century and I dinnae gie a fuck aboot these mental bastards that say different.

It wisnae the swearin I objected tae, no way man, it wis the tone o voice, see. If he had jist says, What the fuck, in a normal sort o voice, and no roared at me – an under-the-breath roar but still a fuckin roar man, wi gritted teeth (and I ken no everybody appreciates that ye can roar wi gritted teeth but I can assure ye, ye can) then, fine, I wida coped wi it like. I widnaea cracked up an screamed, which is what

Tracy says I did and which is why she comes runnin and batterin at the fuckin door.

Luk what ye've fuckin done, ye stupid bastard, the guy Brendan goes, Luk at the fuckin mess, ye stupid bastard ye.

It wis only then I got meself halfway oot the wardrobe an I saw what he mighta meant by the mess, although afterwards I twigged he meant the mental mess as weel. I didnae realise he wis as fucked up as I wis, if not mair, at the time, but I kent whit a mental mess is frae the day I wis born, I think. A bit like Tracy cause the baith o us hus no exactly hud it easy.

The first thing I saw wis the legs an I think (although after the event I'm no totally sure) my first impression wis that this Brendan guy wis screwin some wumman in Forsyth's room and this wis whit he was daein in there. Then I realised the legs belanged tae the auld biddy Forsyth and I thought maybe she'd died o a heart attack after the bastard raped her. I kent she wis deid the minute I saw her face even though I've never seen onybody deid before. It wis a grey colour but it wisnae jist the colour. I never connected the smell till eftir. I mean, it wisnae enough tae make ye boke and, besides, if ye've jist died o a heart attack then ye dinnae smell straightaway, dae ye?

Except she hudnae jist died. I realised when I took in the hale o her, that she couldnae jist be asleep, no in thon position wi her legs skewed apart, plus her eyes were wide open. It dawned on me then the bastard hud come tae put her in a box. The bastard that musta murdered her earlier an then come tae put her in a box an take the body away an dump it where she'll never be fun. He wis even wearin gloves tae carry oot the job. Chop it up likely an then go and dump it in the Clyde, no upriver but − likely oot at sea. Maybe even doon in England where naebody'll ever guess cause if naebody up here ever gied a fuck about the auld biddy as sure as F-U-C-K naebody'll gie a fuck doon there. The folk at the hame were eyewis tellin us how naebody in England gied a fuck aboot us (well, no in so many words but that wis the gist o it) and that wis why folk shouldnae keep runnin aff tae London.

Thank fuck but that Tracy wis at the door because otherwise the guy Brendan for certain sure wis goinae murder me n aw. He had thon murderous look in his eye.

He tried tae keep Tracy at the door even and keep me in even though I wis goin mad tae get away frae him. He hud his haun on my collar and wis pullin at me, near stranglin me, so he wis. Only then Tracy leans forward and bites his haun, like she's half mad, and he falls back and she's in the room.

I thought we were baith goners then for she took wan look at Forsyth laid oot like a lump o stringy meat that had gone aff. I thought she wis goinae puke but instead she sank tae the floor like she'd been battered ower the heid wi a blunt instrument.

She's fainted, the Brendan guy says and bursts into tears again. She fainted and I've done nothin wrong. I come over here because somebody tried to murder me and now luk at me. It's all that wumman Johnson's fault.

I started shiverin. I realised it wis because the room wis freezin as much as the fact that the situation wis creepy, to say the least.

Fiona Ritchie Walker

JACKFRUIT

On the first day of the honey month he buys me jackfruit,
places it on the ledge of our bedroom window.

The same day, while he is working, she phones our home,
says his name, sweet like his mother's tea.

I hear her breath draw back sharp
through her reddened lips as my own voice replies.

On the third day of the honey month I wait for him
to tell me of the letter but his voice stays silent.

The jackfruit sits like a green spiked pig, watching
his empty side of the bed. I count minutes towards daylight.

In our room the smell begins to change. From the ledge
    rises
the warm decay that signals ripe fruit within.

On the tenth day of the honey month he tells me
I am lazy and ungrateful. I have wasted his generous gift.

Its soft, milky moons, fragrant like the nights he promised,
are now rotting round their slimy stones.

Ian Nimmo White

AT THE WATER'S EDGE

The sea wind spins the pebble throwers
round. And much in love they whoop
and clinch. Any chance will do.
A sprinter's dash away,
two tiny figures do much the same,
and their dog, unleashed,
punches like a boxer at the spray,
then takes the ocean head on.

Once they stood here cheek by jowl,
overworked and overdressed,
men in flat caps, women in long skirts
wet at the hem, and children kicking
with their only shoes at tapering water.
They came in droves, leaving the loom,
the crucible, or the pews
on Sundays after dedications.

As the sea magnetically
pulled to and from the land,
they too reined out, reined in,
and with great hollering set themselves
fleetingly, but regularly, free.
Though only gulls now track their line,
I step with deference here today,
a stranger, even to their ghosts.

What do the lovers need to know
of genealogy? What would they care
for ancestors dragged into machines
or all the children who failed to reach five?
The history is short on meaning
if written only in sweat and blood.
Let them catch a thread of gold
in sea, in sun, in laughter.

Ceum air Cheum
by Christopher Whyte

English translation
by Niall O'Gallagher

STEP BY STEP

I

*La tarde en que debía tomar el tren camino de Londres
y Cambridge, dejando al fin Escocia, fui por última vez a
la universidad y, deteniendome en el "quadrangle", miré
bien a todos lados (a la antipatía, lo mismo que a la
simpatía, también puede en algun ocasión complacerle el
demorar la mirada sobre el objecto de ella). Luego me fui.
Rara vez me he ido tan a gusto de sitio alguno.*

LUIS CERNUDA

Did my steps ever touch the steps you left
upon the pavements of the university?
Did my route fall upon the route you took
between the classroom and the library,
from the loneliness of the refectory
to the office where a different, calmer,
safer kind of loneliness was waiting
for us both? Did you take the images

of the few attractive men you saw
and hang them on your memory's four walls,
pictures that stayed clear and radiant
throughout the boredom of each class you taught?
They were so different from the ones you used
to look upon when you still lived in Spain,
a country that you left unwillingly
and where your footsteps never fell again.

How careful did you have to be among
the Scots that sat before you when you taught?
Did you have to watch your steps each time
you went to work among your English colleagues?
Did the fire of suspicion burn
in their eyes from time to time or was
the love you cultivated so exotic,
so impossible, that your desire

Christopher Whyte

CEUM AIR CHEUM

I

La tarde en que debía tomar el tren camino de Londres
y Cambridge, dejando al fin Escocia, fui por última vez a
la universidad y, deteniendome en el "quadrangle", miré
bien a todos lados (a la antipatía, lo mismo que a la
simpatía, también puede en algun ocasión complacerle el
demorar la mirada sobre el objecto de ella). Luego me fui.
Rara vez me he ido tan a gusto de sitio alguno.

LUIS CERNUDA

An do dh'fhairich riamh mo cheumannan do cheum
air cabhsairean an oilthigh? An do lean
mo shlighe fhìn do shlighe, 's sinn a' dol
bho leabharlann gu seòmar-teagaisg, no
bho ionad-bìdh, 's bòrd aonranach ga fhàgail,
gu seòmar pearsant', far am biodh seòrs' eile
a dh'aonranachd a' feitheamh oirnne, ach
nas ciùine, tèarainte? 'S dòcha gu robh

ballachan do sheòmair, ann an lèirsinn
t' inntinn, air an còmhdachadh le dealbhan
nam bòidhchead ainneamh nach do dh'fhairtlich ort
a chruinneachadh rè màirnealachd nan leasan,
's a chumail dìreach, soilleir na do chuimhne.
Bha iad cho eadar-dhealaichte bhon chuid
a bhiodh tu beachdachadh orra san Spàinn,
san tìr mu dheas a dh'fhàg thu gu h-aindèonach,

is far nach fhaighte rithist lorg do cheum.
Chan eil mi cinnteach dè cho faiceallach
's a b' fheudar dhut a bhith nad dhèiligeadh
ris na h-Albannaich sna clasaichean
a bh' agad, air neo ris na Sasannaich
am measg nam fear-teagaisg. An do dheàlraich
lasair amharais bho àm gu àm
'nan sùilean, air neo robh an seòrsa gaoil

could be expressed without danger or shame?
Conscription meant that many lads were missing,
who otherwise would have been in your charge,
and so you had the time to think about
another war that had been lost by both
your people and yourself. As finally
that fruitless war in Spain drew to a close,
and the cause that kept your loyalty

was splitting into petty factions in
the cinema of Stalin's Russian lies,
you were living in a shoddy room
in a hotel in Valencia,
you heard someone knocking on the door
of the next room where your friend was staying
and listened on as he was led away
to be interrogated mercilessly.

It should be no surprise to learn that you
looked upon that second, greater war
with thrawn indifference and a hopelessness
you tried to hide but which was clear enough,
despite your efforts, and condemned. You looked
back to the hidden courtyards of Seville,
that were full of coloured tiles and flowers,
where people sat throughout the summer months,

where nothing living moved under the sun,
until the evening's cool, at last, had come.
Glasgow was different. Week by week the light
would fail in autumn like a candle melting
until the winter's darkness smothered it.
Then you heard the drunkard in your poem
outside pissing on the frozen stones,
of the lane that ran beside your window,

a bha gad àiteachadh cho allmharach,
cho eu-comasach is gum b' urrainnear
do shìor-ghlacadh gun chunnart is gun aire?
Leis a liuthad dhiubh san armailt, leis
a liuthad beàrn am measg nam fiùran òg,
bha gu leòr a dh'ùin' agad airson
smaointinn air cogadh eile, air na chaill
do phoball is na chaill thu fhèin. Air seòmar

dìblidh ann an taigh-òst' am Valencia,
an spàirn gun bhrìgh a' dlùthachadh gu crìoch,
an t-adhbhar 's tus' air taic a chumail ris
a' dol ga bhloighdeachadh, anns an taigh-dhealbh
na breugan Ruiseanach, bualadh san oidhch'
air doras an ath sheòmair, caraid eile
ga chur an sàs 's ga cheasnachadh gun truas.
Cha bu chòir gur adhbhar ioghnaidh dhuinn

nan robh thu sealltainn air an dàrna cogadh
le neo-shùim rag, le eu-dòchas 's tu strì
ri cheiltinn, ach a mhothaicheadh neach dha,
a mhothaich is a dhìt. Bhiodh tus' a' coimhead
air ais gu cùirtean falaichte am baile
t' àraich, a bha làn de fhlùraichean
's crèadh-leacan datht', daoine 'nan suidhe ann,
's an teas eu-tròcaireach, gun ghluasad beòthail

fad feasgair samhraidh, ann an camhanaich
's e meallt', a' feitheamh air an oidhche fhìor.
Bha Glaschu diofaraicht'. Seachdain air sheachdain,
an leus a' fàilneachadh as t-fhoghar, mar
gur coinneal e ga cathadh beag is beag
gus na mhùchadh leis an duibhre i.
Chual' thu 'n uair sin, air taobh eile t' uinneig,
misgear a' mùn air clachan reòtht' na lònaid

about eleven in an echo of
the heavy downpour that prevented you
from reading when you sat on other nights
with just your trusty lamp for company.
You had no love for this cruel, northern place
or for its university, the two
went hand in hand, two punishments that you
were sentenced to, in exile, for three years.

You had been banished from the place you loved
and made to live there in the company
of strangers whom you could not understand.
But your years in Glasgow weren't in vain,
because you wrote a book of poetry
as perfect as you wrote throughout your life.
You praised beauty in clean and sober words
that left us proof of your great artistry.

a bhruidhinn thu mu dheidhinn na do dhàin,
fuaim san oidhch' mu thimcheall aon uair deug,
mar ath-aithris air dòrtadh trom nan sian
a bhac do leughadh air oidhcheannan eil',
's tu gun chompanach ach lampa dhìleas.
Cha robh gaol agad air a' bhaile seo
air neo air oilthigh, bha e dùbailte,
am fògradh bha 'na bhinn dhut rè trì bliadhna.

'S tu fuadaichte bho àiteachan do ghaoil,
b' fheudar dhut fuireachd am measg shrainnsearan
nach tuigeadh tu 'n dòigh, 's nach do thuig do chràdh.
Ach cha robh do bhliadhnaichean an Glaschu
gun fheum, 's tu cur ri chèile leabhar dhàn
cho coileanta 's a rinn thu fad do bheatha.
Mhol thu gach bòidhchead an cainnt chaisgte, ghlain
is dh'fhàg thu dhuinne teisteanas air t' ealain.

II

... joyeux de fuir une patrie infâme

CHARLES BAUDELAIRE

I have no more love than you had for
that place, though I was born a short while from
the university, though I grew up
even closer still, though I returned
after fifteen years to teach the native
literature. When I was a boy and then
a teenager my steps never crossed your steps.
I avoided the university,

and had no reason to go there since you
had quit the place long before I was born.
While I travelled between the house and
the school, or between the school, the library
and the church, I sometimes used to think
that I was treading on the border that
seperated madness from sanity.
And so that city gradually became

a mental scenery, a spiritual
symbol of a thing that I could not
make sense of, a mystery that settled
inside me, but came between my eyes
and every labour that I contemplated.
Indeed, some mornings after I woke up
I was afraid that when I put my foot
upon the bedroom carpet I would travel

in that domain of madness, that the city
would have metamorphosed completely.
I could not love the place where I was born
although when I came back I was equipped
with every tool of reason and of knowledge
that I needed to reveal the mystery
or to be an enchanter and cast out,
if I had to, every demon in the place.

II

... joyeux de fuir une patrie infâme
CHARLES BAUDELAIRE

Chan eil nas mò de ghaol agamsa air,
am baile sin, na na bha agad fhèin,
ged nach do rugadh mi ach astar beag
air falbh bhon oilthigh, ged a chaidh mo thogail
na b' fhaisge fhathast air, is ged a thill mi
air ais aig ceann còig bliadhna deug, chun
an litreachas bha dùthchasach a theagasg.
Is mi 'nam bhalach no 'nam dheugaire,

cha deach mo cheumannan trast air do cheum.
Sheachain mi 'n t-oilthigh, cha robh adhbhar agam
a bhith dol ann, 's tus' air an t-àite thrèigsinn
fada mus deach mo bhreith. Is mise siubhal
eadar an taigh 's an sgoil, no eadar an sgoil,
an leabharlann 's an eaglais, smaoinichinn
uaireannan gur ann a dh'iomall tìr
na cuthaich bha mo cheumannan a' beantainn.

Mar sin bha 'm baile, beag is beag, a' fàs
'na dhealbh-choltas inntinneil, 'na shamhladh
spioradail air rud a dh'fhairtlich orm
a chur an cèill, air dìomhaireachd a dh'àitich
a-staigh orm, ach a choinnicheadh mo shùil
's gach gnothach a bhiodh i beachdachadh air.
Dìreach, bha maidnean ann, an dèidh dhomh dùsgadh,
bha eagal ormsa, nuair a bheanadh bonn

mo choise ri brat-ùrlair 'n t-seòmar-cadail,
gur ann an tìr na cuthaich shiùbhlainn-sa,
's cruth-atharrachadh a' bhail' air tighinn gu buil.
Cha b' urrainn gaol a bhith agam air,
ged a thill mi air ais 's gach ball-acainn
a th' aig an reusan is an tuigse deasaicht'
gus an dìomhaireachd a nochdadh, neo
gu bhith 'nam gheasadair, nam biodh e feumail

That was impossible. But I discovered
another dilemma, a conceptual
mystery. Teaching was a battle,
not between the students and the man
or woman that stood before them or sat
among them, but between the teaching staff
themselves. Teaching was to me a way of
learning, playing with concepts and ideas,

that glanced and glimpsed and splashed around the room
until there were so many that you had
no clear idea of which one you should choose
with which to start again and even then
you could not predict your destination
with so many paths open in your mind.
But there were others for whom teaching was
a means of domination or possession,

of erecting boundaries and imposing
their definitions on the land, on words
and even on an individual book.
Playfulness was foreign to that lot,
and many of the students that I taught,
were attracted to their way of thinking.
And so the freedom that I had at first
gradually began to fall away,

and restrictions started to appear
on the ways that people thought or even
on their freedom to express themselves.
Those other teachers loved their definitions,
especially of words connected to
the country and the people who lived there;
they liked to prescribe limits on the ways
that Scottish people looked upon the world

deamhain uil' an àit' a chur mu sgaoil.
Bha sin do-dhèanta. Agus na nochdadh leam,
b' e imcheist eile e, no dìomhaireachd
bun-bheachdail, oir bha 'n teagasg 'na bhlàr-catha,
chan ann eadar na h-oileanaich 's am fear
no 'm boireannach a bha 'na sheasamh romhpa,
air neo 'na shuidhe anns a' mheadhan, ach
eadar na fir-theagaisg fhèin. B' e dòigh

air ionnsachadh a chunnaic mi san teagasg,
cluiche le bun-bheachdan 's beachdan-bharail,
a' plathadh is a' boillsgeadh is a' stealladh
gus am bitheadh uiread dhiubh san t-seòmar
's nach robh fhios agad dè am fear bu chòir dhut
roghainn airson toiseachadh às ùr,
no dè an seòladh anns an rachadh tu
's a leithid a shlighean fosgailte nad inntinn.

Ach bha cuid ann 's an teagasg, air an sgàth,
'na dhòigh air ceannsachadh no seilbheachadh,
air crìochan a stèidheachadh 's air an dligh'
a bh' aca ghlaodhadh air fearann, air facal,
dìreach air leabhar àraidh. Cha robh a' chluich
a' còrdadh ris a' chuid seo idir, is
bha 'm modh a bh' aca tarraingeach airson
feadhainn am measg nan oileanach, airson

buidheann nach gann. Mar sin bha an t-saorsa
a bh' agam nuair a thòisich mi a' dol
ga lùghdachadh, is bacaidhean a' nochdadh
air dòighean-smaoineachaidh no dòighean-labhairt.
B' ionmhainn leotha sònrachadh a dhèanamh,
gu h-àraidh air faclan a bhuineadh ris
an dùthaich 's ris na daoin' a bha beò ann:
shocair iad mar a bu chòir Albannach

and spilt ink laying down exactly what
they held the meaning of "Scottish" to be.
I only gradually understood
that their pedantry and their precision
always meant someone would be shut out,
and that when they'd put up their boundaries
I would end up, more often than not, on
the wrong side of the fence. This didn't make

me angry, simply puzzled and perplexed.
I was born in that place, grew up there,
the place where I first learned of suffering,
and they could say that I did not belong?
Was it only the kind of love that dwelt
inside me, or that I used Latin when
I prayed and sang hymns to the Creator,
when I was no more than a little boy?

a shealltainn air an t-saoghal, air neo dìreach
dè bha 'na chèill don fhacal "Albannach".
Cha do thuig mi ach beag is beag gu robh
dùnadh a-mach 'na bhuaidh do-sheachainte
aig gach uile phongalachd a bh' aca
is mise, mar as trice, air an taobh
cheàrr dhen fheansa, nuair a bha a' chrìoch
stèidhichte leò. Cha b' e adhbhar feirge

air mo shon an obrachadh, ach adhbhar
imcheist. Rugadh mise anns an àite,
chaidh mo thogail 's mo phianadh an sin,
is theireadh neach nach robh mi buntainn dha?
Chan ann a-mhàin a thaobh an t-seòrsa gaoil
a dh'àitich mi, ach chionn 's gur anns an Laidinn
a ghuidhinn-sa, is mi 'nam phàiste beag,
's a sheinninn-sa laoidhean a' Chruthadair?

III

*S fonarem obshar'te
ves podlunnyj svet!
Toj strany na karte —
net, v prostranstve — net.*

MARINA TSVETAEVA*

You left Glasgow for Cambridge before leaving
Cambridge for the New World where at last
you found yourself a home in Mexico.
You would never see Seville again
but all around you, in a way that was
both foreign and familiar, your language
was spoken day by day. The words you found
for the country that you'd left were harsh.

You thought the language to which you were chained
and which you had to write in was a curse.
You said a poet couldn't choose his background,
his country or his language but must keep
the highest and most perfect loyalty
to his conscience only. He must write
not for the countrymen assigned to him
by a cruel and bitter fate but for

whoever listened with a ready mind
and a generous understanding,
whatever language they used, whatever
country they belonged to. Should the words
that I use when I speak about my country
be gentler, my little northern homeland?
The homeland that for me was never homely,
where I never was or will be protected?

---

* But another quotation from Tsvetaeva would be so appropriate here: "Tak
kraj menja ne uberëg/ moj shto i samyj zorkyj syshik/ vdol' vsej dushi, vsej
poperëk/ rodimovo pjatna ne syshet!"

III

S fonarem obshar'te
ves podlunnyj svet!
Toj strany na karte —
net, v prostranstve — net.

MARINA TSVETAEVA*

Dh'fhàg thu Glaschu airson Cambridge, Cambridge
airson an t-Saoghail Ùir is, aig a' cheann
thall, fhuair thu dachaigh ann am Mexico.
Chan fhacas rithist leat baile Seville,
ach mun cuairt ort, an dòigh nach robh co-ionann
ach nach robh dìreach coigreach, bha do chànain
ga bruidhinn là seach là. Fhuair thusa faclan
ro chruaidh airson na tìr a dh'fhàg thu. B' e

dìreach mallachd a chunnaic thu sa chànain
a bha gad cheangal rithe, is a dh'fheum thu
sgrìobhadh innte. Cha b' urrainn do bhàrd,
thuirt thu, a dhualchas no a thìr a roghainn,
air neo a chànain, ach bu chòir gu robh
an dìlseachd a b' àirde 's a bu shàir a bh' aige
da chogais fhèin a-mhàin. Bu chòir dha sgrìobhadh,
chan ann airson nan co-fhear-dùthch' a shònraich

an dàn ('s e magail, searbh) dha, ach airson
na bhiodh ag èisteachd ris le aigne dheiseil
is tuigse làin, ge b' e a' chànain bha
ga cleachdadh leò, ge b' e 'n tìr dan do bhuin iad.
Am bu chòir dhaibh a bhith nas maoith', na faclan
a chleachdar leams' an uair a bhruidhneas mi
mu mo thìr fhìn, mo dhùthaich bheag mu thuath?
Mu dhùthaich air mo shon nach dùthchasail,

---

* Ach bitheadh earrann eile bho Tsvetaeva cho freagarrach anns an àite seo:
"Tak kraj menja ne uberëg/ moj shto i samyj zorkyj syshik/ vdol' vsej dushi,
vsej poperëk/ rodimovo pjatna ne syshet!"

Because every family is a little
country of its own and immigrants
live in its midst as they do everywhere.
The longest living of my mother's sisters
spent her last days in an old folks' home.
They said that she was senile but I think
that she was very lucid when she said
the people all around her were "so Scottish".

She was born, just as my mother was,
near Glasgow and had never lived in Ireland,
but the country where they had been born,
where they were brought up and where they lived,
was a place of exile in their eyes,
surrounded by strangers and enemies.
They did not imagine the hostility
that they felt around them when they were

just infants and young girls. How can I make
sense of the feeling that my mother had,
of her relationship to her own city,
her foreignness at the heart of her own
country? I cannot untie that knot,
the knot that is so tangled and so tight.
Glasgow was an impossibility
to me, a place that you could visit but

which you had to leave to start anew.
I didn't understand how Glasgow could
be homely, all I ever felt there was
disconnectedness, or even exile.
I felt jealousy towards those who
felt as connected to valleys and mountains
as if they were parts of their bodies.
Envy, indecision and great longing.

dùthaich far nach do dhìonadh mi 's nach dìonar?
Oir tha gach teaghlach 'na dhùthaich bhìg fhèin,
is bidh eilthirich beò 'na mheadhan cuideachd.
De pheathraichean mo mhàthar, chuir an tè
as fhaid bha beò a lathaichean mu dheireadh
seachad ann an taigh nan daoine aosta.
Bha i letheach às a ciall, ach b' e
's dòch' an abairt a bu thùrail' thàinig

bho bilean gu robh na daoine chunnaic i
mu thimcheall oirre "dìreach Albannach".
Rugadh i, mar a rugadh mo mhàthair,
faisg air Glaschu, cha robh iad riamh fuireachd
an Èirinn, ach bha tìr am breith 's an àraich
'na h-àite-fògraidh 'na an sùilean, 's iad
cuairtichte le nàimhdean 's srainnsearan.
Cha b' obair a' mhic-mheanmna e an nàimhdeas

a dh'fhairich iad mun cuairt orra is iad
'nam pàistean no 'nan caileagan. Ciamar
a chuireas mi an cèill an fhaireachdainn
a bh' aig mo mhàthair, dàimh-se ris a' bhaile,
h-an-dùthchasachd an crìdh' a dùthcha fhèin?
Cha tèid an snaidhm sin fhuasgladh leam, is e
cho iomadh-fhillte, teann. Air mo shon fhìn
b' e do-dhèantachd a bh' ann an Glaschu, àite

a thriallar ann is far nach urrainnear
ach astar ùr a thòiseachadh. Cha robh
mi tuigsinn mar a dh'fhaodadh Glaschu bhith
dùthchasail, cha robh na ghabhadh ann ach
do-bhuntainn, dìreach fuadachadh gu tur.
Bha tnù agam ri neach a dh'fhairicheas
srath, sliabh no coille mar bhall a chuirp fhèin.
Tnù, iomachomhairle is ionndrainn mhòr.

IV

Segíts szabadság,
ó hadd leljem meg végre honnomat!

MIKLÓS RADNÓTI

Ne v tom sut' zhizni, shto v nej jest,
no v vere v to, shto v nej dolzhno byt'.

JOSEPH BRODSKY

Freedom, can you help me, or should I turn
to another of the abstract notions
created by the human mind to people
the emptiness that it feels and fears?
Can you show me my home, the homely earth
that has always eluded me 'til now?
Can you be more use to me than to
that poet* they condemned because of his

Jewish blood, as their laws defined it,
and with which they oppressed him 'til he died?
What can I say about my own blood?
Should I say the blood flowing through my veins
is Protestant and not just Catholic?
Would that protect me, keep me on the right path?
But how can anybody say that blood
has a religion, or different dogmas,

or any task except to carry oxygen
to the different members of our bodies,
to bring colour to our cheeks and throb
against our temples? He didn't want to be
a Jew, his customs, his religion and
his language were those of his countrymen.
How could anyone accurately
describe the blood, the seed of such a man?

* Miklós Radnóti (1909–1944).

IV

Segíts szabadság,
ó hadd leljem meg végre honnomat!

MIKLÓS RADNÓTI

Ne v tom sut' zhizni, shto v nej jest,
no v vere v to, shto v nej dolzhno byt'.

JOSEPH BRODSKY

A shaorsa, am bi thu gam chuideachadh,
air neo tè eile de na cùis-bheachdan
a dh'innlich inntinn dhaonna gus an fhailmhe
mhothaich i dhà, 's a bha cur eagal oirre,
phoblachadh? An seall thu dhomh mo thalamh
dùthchasail, mo dhachaigh fhìn mu dheireadh?
An nochdar thu nas fheumaile dhomh fhìn
na nochd do bhàrd* a chaidh dhìteadh air sgàth

na fala Iùdhaich, mar a shònraich iad,
's a shàraicheadh leò gus na chaochail e?
Dè na their mi air cuspair m' fhala fhìn?
An abair mi gur Pròstanach na shileas
trom chuisleanan, 's nach Caitligeach a-mhàin?
'M bu dòigh sin air mo cheartachadh no m' dhìonadh?
Ach dè mar a dh'fhaodas creideamh a bhith
aig an fhuil, no deifir theagasgan a bhith

aice, no dreuchd eil' ach ocsaidean
a thoirt do bhuill ar cuirp, rudhadh aiseag
dar gruaidhean, 's bualadh seasmhach dar leth-chinn?
Cha robh e 'g iarraidh bhith 'na Iùdhach, 's e
a' leantainn dòigh 's creideamh a cho-fhear-dhùthcha,
's a' cleachdadh an aon chànain. Cò tha ann
a mhìnicheas gu ceart an fhìrinneachd
mu dheidhinn fuil a' bhàird ud, is a shìl?

---

* Miklós Radnóti (1909–1944).

What was in his mind each time he wished
to step upon the ground of his true homeland?
I don't think that he held out any hope
for sudden change to come upon the country
that had denounced and banished him, that made
him wear a yellow star upon his arm,
a star with meaning in the eyes of some
but to which he was indifferent.

His country was a faith he carried with him,
a hope he clung to everywhere he went,
the image of a woman's body, maybe,
her thighs, her breasts, or the memory of
the last normal day they spent together,
sitting at his desk, his last cigarette
between his lips, that sweetness half-rotten,
pre-echoing those famous lines of his,

his wife waiting for him in the bed,
her body's heat while she slept at his side,
a pencil in his fingers' grip while he
kept playing with the lazy syllables
of that precious line that he could not
organise at all, struggling with
that line and with the sleep on his eyelids.
But there was more in home that he desired,

a freedom of meaning, escape from labels,
from oppressive fixed definitions,
the names that come like bullets that must be
avoided for as long as possible.
That place was not one that had been established,
that home, nor was it a place where you could
stop and take a rest, but closer to a
space, a journey, renewing every meaning.

Dè bha 'na inntinn nuair a dhùraig e
a bhith ceumnachadh talamh a fhìor-dùthcha?
Chan eil mi smaoineachadh gu robh dùil aig'
grad-atharrachadh thighinn air an dùthaich
a rinn a chàineadh is a dh'fhuadaich e,
cho-èignich e gus reul bhuidhe a ghiùlan
a bha ciall aice ann an sùilean feadhna,
ach gun chèill idir aic' air a shon fhèin.

B' e seòrsa creideimh bha 'na dhachaigh aige,
dòchas a chumadh taic ris anns gach àite,
cuimhn' air bodhaig boireannaich, math dh'fhaodte,
a sliasaidean, a cìochan, no air uair
anmoch latha gnàthaichte, is e
'na shuidhe aig a dheasg, toitean mu dheireadh
eadar a bhilean, a' mhìls' ud leth-ghrod,
ro-mhothachadh do loidhnean aithnichte

a chèile a bha feitheamh air san leabaidh,
da teas is i, 's dòcha, 'na cadal cheana,
peansail ann an glac a mheòirean, 's e
fhathast a' cluich le lidean faoin na loidhn'
a b' annsa leis, nach gabhadh riaghladh leis
air dòigh sam bith, agus esan a' strì
rithe 's ri cadalachd a fhabhrannan.
Ach bha nas mò san dachaigh dhùraig e:

saorsadh nan ciall, fuasgladh bho chomharraidhean,
bho shuaicheantasan sònraicht', èiginneach,
na h-ainmean a thig mar pheilearan
a dh'fheumas neach an seachnadh fhad 's a ghabhar.
Cha b' e àite stèidhichte a bh' innt',
an dachaigh sin, no far am b' urrainnear
stad is dàil a dhèanamh, 's i nas coltaich'
ri astar, siubhal, ùrachadh gach cèill.

Perhaps that place was just a dream that he
took with him, just a possibility
embracing the connections that exist
between things and their names, connecting
person to person. There'd be no sense
in grasping them and firing them like weapons.
Someone would open his closed fist to see
what had been lying hidden in the palm

of his hand (without knowing in advance
the purport of what had been hidden there)
and show it to his friend. That land had been
inhabited by people that were just,
hardy and, above all, tolerant.
Unless we put together verses that
are regular, and with the faith that they
will find readers, responsive and open,

some, perhaps, who haven't yet been born,
we won't be working or labouring
effectively without being connected
already to that nation, to that land,
although our feet will never touch its soil
as long as we're alive. Nobody can
be banished from that country, that welcomes
every exile and every exile's language.

Language can't be inhabited because
language is a bridge. It can't protect
anyone from real, physical bullets.
A bullet reached the poet's heart and he
was buried in the soil of strangers.
But his words did not stay in the grave:
their fate was not to be control or exile,
but journeying and meaning once again.

Edinburgh and Pest,
September 2004 – March 2006

Cha robh i ach 'na bhruadar aige, 's dòcha,
a bha dol còmhla ris mar so-dhèantachd,
a' beantainn ris na ceanglan a bhios ann
eadar cùisean 's ainmeannan, is eadar
duin' is duin'. Cha bhiodh na cèill, an sin,
gan glacadh is gan losgadh mar bhuill-airm.
Dh'fhosgladh neach a dhòrn-san dùinte, mar
gum b' ann, airson na bha ga cheiltinn air

bos a làimh a nochdadh dhà fhèin (bho
nach biodh fhios aige ro-làimh air a bhrìgh)
is ri a charaid, cuideachd. Bha i air
a poblachadh, an dachaigh sin, le daoine
cearta, fulangaich is ceadachail.
Mura tèid rann sam bith a chur ri chèil'
tha riaghailteach, ach creideamh a bhith ann
gum faigh e leughadairean freagarraich,

feadhainn, math dh'fhaodte, nach eil fhathast ann,
cha bhi sinn 'g obrachadh no gnìomhachadh
gu h-èifeachdach gun a bhith buntainn rithe,
an dachaigh sin, an nàisean sin, a cheana,
ged nach beanadh bonn ar cois da h-ùir
cho fad 's a tha sinn beò. Chan urrainn neach
bhith fuadaichte bhon dùthaich sin, a chuireas
fàilt' air gach fògarrach is air a chànain.

Cha ghabh cànain àiteachadh, oir 's e
drochaid a th' innte. Chan fhaod i a bharrachd
neach a dhìon bho pheilear fìrinneach.
Ràinig peilear uchd a' bhàird, is bha
e tiodhlaicht' ann an ùir aig srainnsearan.
Ach cha do dh'fhan fhaclan-san anns an uaigh,
cha do dh'aithnich iad srian no fògarrachd,
no dàn ach siubhal 's ciallachadh as ùr.

                              Dùn Èideann agus Pest,
                    an t-Sultain 2004 — am Mart 2006

BIOGRAPHIES

Keith Aitchison lives and works in Inverness. He writes chiefly during winter, when darkness and poor weather bring the urge to make stories. These usually have their beginning in something seen or heard, may finish as mostly recollection, or wholly fiction, so long as they entertain.

Kirsten Anderson is 29 and lives in Glasgow. She is a recent graduate of the University of Glasgow's MLitt in Creative Writing and has had stories published in *Outside of a Dog* and *The Dreaming City: Glasgow 2020 and the Power of Mass Imagination*.

Dorothy Baird lives in Edinburgh where she works as a Human Givens therapist and facilitates creative writing groups for adults and children. Her poems have been widely published in magazines and anthologies and her first collection, *Leaving the Nest*, will be published by Two Ravens Press in the summer of 2007.

David Betteridge: a teacher and teacher-trainer, has been writing since the 1960s. Poems and poem-sequences include *Found* (an elegy for the crew of the Solway Harvester), *May Day* (where the world comes to Glasgow Green), *Boogying* (where Nelson Mandela comes to George Square), and *Climbing Beinn Dobhrain* (in praise of Duncan Ban MacIntyre).

Norman Bissell is a different man from the one whose poems appeared in *NWS* 24. He's still from Glasgow and his work's been widely published, but he's moving to the Isle of Luing to write full-time. His first collection, *Slate, Sea and Sky*, with photographs by Oscar Marzaroli, is to be published by Luath Press and he's writing a non-fiction book.

Eunice M. Buchanan was born and brought up in Arbroath. After studies at Edinburgh University and training college she became a Primary School teacher. On retiral she attended Creative Writing evening classes at Glasgow University where she is currently working on a PhD.

Maoilios Caimbeul/Myles Campbell is from Skye with Lewis connections. His publications include *Saoghal Ùr* (diehard 2003) and *Breac-a'-Mhuiltein* (Coiscéim, Dublin 2007), a Gaelic/Gaeilge bilingual collection that includes most of his poetry since 1974. *Dreuchd an Fhigheadair — The Weavers's Task: a Gaelic Sampler* (Scottish Poetry Library 2007) includes two poems with 'responses' by John Burnside and Jackie Kay.

Jim Carruth was born in Johnstone in 1963. He has two collections of poetry published. *High Auchensale* (Ludovic Press 2006) is the second part of a longer sequence started with *Bovine Pastoral* (Ludovic Press 2004). He is a founding member and current chair of St Mungo's Mirrorball and a committee member of the Stanza poetry festival.

Alison Craig was born and miseducated in Birmingham, before moving to Scotland in 1981. She writes poetry, fiction, articles and book reviews. Living and working in Ayrshire, she has a nearly-three-year-old daughter. She still marvels at the sea, after early years in a concrete jungle.

Born in Shetland, in 1947, **John Cumming** grew up in a fishing and crofting family. After studying sculpture and ceramics at Gray's School of Art, he taught in Aberdeen and Fife. In 1979 he moved to Stromness, Orkney, where he now works full time as a sculptor.

Lesley Dargie is from Aberdeen and has a degree in English Literature. She became a nurse and has worked as a Health Visitor for 26 years. A husband and four children have hindered 'The Novel' but the 2006 OU Creative Writing course produced some poems and this is her first publication.

Derenz, born in Annan in the 1950s, lives and writes in Alloa. Derenz enjoys exploring all forms of writing including poetry, stage and screenplays, and rises to the challenge of public performance. The publication of the short story *Forbidden Strangers* is a first for Derenz.

Andrew Elliott lives in Glasgow. He is working on a collection of poems.

Raymond Friel (*The Flask*): born in Greenock in 1963. Graduated from Glasgow University, moved to England and qualified as a teacher. Poetry collections include *Seeing the River* (1995) and *A World Fit to Live In* (2006). Lives in Somerset with his wife and three sons. Currently headteacher of a secondary school in Bath.

Raymond Friel (*An American Hitman in Glasgow*) is a 32-year-old screenwriter born and working in Glasgow. Credits include *The Calcium Kid* and *Botched* (released later this year). *Moriarty Is Crying* (a play) was performed at the Edinburgh Festival and the Citizens' Theatre in Glasgow in 2005. Proud father of three-month-old Rémy.

Graham Fulton has been writing poetry for 20 years. His collections include *Humouring the Iron Bar Man* (Polygon), *This* (Rebel Inc), *Knights of the Lower Floors* (Polygon), *Ritual Soup and other liquids* (Mariscat). Two new collections, *Upside Down Heart* and *Black Motel*, are to be published by Dreadful Night Press.

Valerie Gillies is the Edinburgh Makar, poet laureate to the city. Her most recent books are *Men and Beasts* (2000) and *The Lightning Tree* (2002). She received a Creative Scotland Award to write *The Spring Teller* (forthcoming), which is a book of landmark poems inspired by Scotland's wells and springs.

Australian by passport, **Merryn Glover** was born in Kathmandu, brought up in Nepal, India and Pakistan, and now calls Scotland home. She has a growing body of stories published and broadcast on radio and is working on a novel. Other jobs have included teaching, community arts and hoovering.

Paul Gorman's work has appeared in *Cutting Teeth*, *Pulp.Net* and *New Writing Scotland 23* and *24*, among others. Shortlisted for the 2002 Dundee Book Prize, he is currently taking a very long time to write a dark fantasy novel for children. He is married and lives in Midlothian.

Kate Hendry teaches in prisons and for the Open

University. Her stories have appeared in *Harpers*, *New Writing Scotland* and *Mslexia*, amongst others. Last year she received an Arts Council Bursary to write the first draft of a novel. She lives in Ayrshire with her partner, son, hens and ducks.

Vicki Husband has been published in the National Museums of Scotland anthology *Present Poets* and *Aesthetica* magazine. Vicki was brought up in Edinburgh and is now settled in Glasgow although she came a very long way round via Carlisle, Hull, Norway, Greece, Eastbourne and Brighton.

Fiona Jack was born and brought up in Anstruther, a fishing village in Fife. She's lived in Sheffield with her family for many years, but misses the sea and the beaches of 'Anster', and returns to Scotland frequently. The poets she most cares about are Burns, Keats and Bob Dylan.

Andy Jackson was born in Manchester in 1965, but moved to Scotland in 1992, now living in north-east Fife. He works for Dundee University, and this is his debut appearance in *New Writing Scotland*.

Mary Johnston *née* Mackie, brought up in rural Aberdeenshire now lives in Midlothian. She considers herself bi-lingual – Doric her first language, forbidden when she started school. She has published two pamphlets of poems: *Teuchat Storm*, a collection of early childhood memories, and *Smaa Spangs*, translations of German Lieder into Doric.

Helen Lamb has published a poetry collection, *Strange Fish*, and a short story collection, *Superior Bedsits* (Polygon). Her work has also been widely published in literary journals and anthologies. Many of her stories have been broadcast on radio. She is currently a Royal Literary Fund fellow at Edinburgh University.

Louise Laurie was born in North Ayrshire. She has lived throughout the UK and the Middle East. Her first poetry collection was *Sweeping Away The Rain*. She has been published in various anthologies, including Scottish Cultural Press. She lives in South Ayrshire and is currently writing a crime novel.

Peter Maclaren taught English in Glasgow schools between 1971 and 2005. Wrote a regular column in *TESS* until a new editor spiked his copy. Has had poems in *Lines Review*, *Akros*, *Teaching English*, *Glasgow Review*, *Glasgow English Magazine* and *Cencrastus*. (How come so many of these magazines are defunct?)

Ciara MacLaverty was born in Belfast in 1968 and has lived in Scotland most of her life. Previous stories have appeared in *NWS* 15 and 16. A poem entitled 'Peeled', from her first pamphlet *Seats for Landing*, was selected among the Best Scottish Poems of 2006. Her blog can be found at **www.ciaramaclaverty.co.uk**.

Sandra McQueen was born and raised in Dundee, although her family roots are in Fife. She has had a few poems and short stories published in literary magazines, been commended in the National Portrait Gallery's first poetry competition last year and was twice shortlisted in the McCash Scots Poetry competition.

Andy Manders lives in Perthshire, writing the odd bit poem and story when looking after the bairns, earning a meagre crust and weather permit.

Lynsey May lives, loves and writes in Edinburgh.

Theresa Muñoz is a second generation Filipino-Canadian born in Vancouver, British Columbia. She is a graduate of the MLitt in Creative Writing course at the University of Glasgow. She presently resides in Glasgow under the Fresh Talent: Working in Scotland Scheme. Her fiction and poetry have appeared in *The Claremont Review*, *Room of One's Own* and *Canadian Literature*.

Donald S. Murray comes from the Isle of Lewis but teaches in Shetland. Widely published, some of his work – both short stories and poetry – has been shortlisted for national awards. His forthcoming book of verse *Speak To Us, Catriona* is based on the tales and traditions of Lewis and published by the Islands Book Trust.

Andrew Nicoll has worked on Scottish daily newspapers since 1980. Born and brought up in Dundee, he now covers the Scottish Parliament for the *Sun*. He's been writing fiction for the past five years and has a novel sitting in a drawer at home. **asnicoll@yahoo.co.uk**

Niall O'Gallagher is a writer, musician and journalist. He was shortlisted for the McCash Prize for Scots poetry 2006 and in the Gaelic section of the Wigtown Poetry Prize 2006. His criticism, journalism and translations have appeared in publications including *Gath*, *The Herald* and *New Writing Scotland*. Niall stays in Glasgow where he works for BBC Craoladh nan Gaidheal.

Tom Pow's latest publications are *Transfusion* – a poem in praise of Muhammad Ali and Nelson Mandela – (Shoestring Press) and *Captives* (Corgi). In 2007 he received a Creative Scotland Award. He teaches creative writing and storytelling at Glasgow University Crichton Campus in Dumfries.

Originally from Oldham, **Heather Reid** moved to Scotland as an adult and trained to be a social worker at Aberdeen University. She currently lives in Perthshire with her husband, two sons and a guide dog puppy. She is a member of the Soutar House writers group.

Alan Riach is Professor of Scottish Literature at Glasgow University. His fourth book of poems, *Clearances* (2001), follows *First & Last Songs* (1995), *An Open Return* (1991) and *This Folding Map* (1990). His radio series *The Good of the Arts*, first broadcast in New Zealand in 2001, may be visited at **www.southwest.org.nz**

Dilys Rose lives in Edinburgh. She writes mostly poetry, fiction and, recently, libretti, and enjoys collaborating with visual artists and musicians. She has published ten books, most recently *Lure* (poetry), *Lord of Illusions* (short stories) and *Selected Stories*. A new collection of poems, *Bodywork*, is forthcoming. She is currently working on two librettos, *Helter Skelter* (music theatre) and *The Child of Europe* (chamber opera). **dilysrose.com**

Hester Ross is from the Oa, Islay and lives in Leith. She lived with her family in Malawi for eleven years, latterly teaching Literature at Chancellor College. She graduated MSc in Creative Writing from Edinburgh University last year, is working on her first novel, and plotting a return to Islay.

Cherise Saywell grew up in Australia and has lived in Scotland for eleven years. She has published short stories in *The London Magazine* and *Carvezine*, and won the VS Pritchett Prize in 2003. She was awarded an SAC Bursary in the same year, and is currently wrestling with a novel.

Alexis Scott was born and brought up in Derry, Northern Ireland. Living in Scotland for more than 30 of the past 33 years. First novel *Eating Wolves* published by Dewi Lewis, 2003. Articles in the *Times Educational Supplement Scotland*, short stories in *Northwords* and *The Stinging Fly*.

Fiona Ritchie Walker is from Montrose, Angus, now living in Blaydon, near Newcastle. She writes poetry, short stories and plays. Her latest poetry collections are *Garibaldi's Legs* (Iron Press) and the chapbook *Angus Palette* (Sand), which is illustrated by her sister, Kirsten Ritchie Walker. **www.fionaritchiewalker.co.uk**

Ian Nimmo White is a prolifically published poet who was a youth and community worker with Fife Council for 35 years. Writes in both English and Scots and has produced three collections of poetry: *Memory and Imagination* (Scottish Book Trust 1998), *Standing Back* (Petrel 2002) and *Symmetry* (Trafford, due out in summer 2007).

Christopher Whyte's third collection *Dealbh Athar* will be published by Coiscéim of Dublin. A prize-winning poet in Gaelic and the author of four novels in English, he taught from 1990 to 2005 in the Department of Scottish Literature at Glasgow University. He now lives in Budapest and writes full-time.